JOHN SIMMONS

WE, ME, THEM &IT

HOW TO WRITE POWERFULLY FOR BUSINESS

21ST ANNIVERSARY EDITION

Published by
LID Publishing
An imprint of LID Business Media Ltd.
The Record Hall, Studio 304,
16-16a Baldwins Gardens,
London EC1N 7RJ, UK

info@lidpublishing.com
www.lidpublishing.com

A member of:

BPR ✸

businesspublishersroundtable.com

Printed by Gutenberg Press, Malta
ISBN: 978-1-911687-00-9
ISBN: 978-1-911687-01-6 (ebook)

Cover design: Caroline Li
Page design: David Carroll & Co

JOHN SIMMONS

WE, ME, THEM & IT

HOW TO WRITE POWERFULLY FOR BUSINESS

21ST ANNIVERSARY EDITION

MADRID | MEXICO CITY | LONDON
NEW YORK | BUENOS AIRES
BOGOTA | SHANGHAI | NEW DELHI

Contents

Foreword

I have always believed in the life-changing impact of certain books. Great authors can inspire, educate and create change. I am a greedy, voracious reader so have read many fiction and non-fiction books across the years. From them all, there are only a tiny number I would list as ones that have actually created a dramatic change in the way I think or have transformed the way I work. This book is, without doubt, on that list.

At the start of my career, I received a 'classical' brand management training at Procter & Gamble and Coca-Cola. I learnt about some of the science and principles of brands, marketing and business. We thought a lot about 'communication', both to the customer and inside the business – but there was never a specific focus on the power of language.

I then joined Interbrand, the global brand agency that had done much to shape the way business understood branding. John Simmons was there; an established figure, running a department I didn't really understand but was intrigued by. He had called it Verbal Identity: a way to demonstrate a natural and equal relationship between the visual and verbal elements of a brand. The visual elements – logo, colours, images, typography – were easily spotted. But how do brands communicate if they don't use words? It was a question that brand consultancies needed to address fully but had chosen to ignore.

We, Me, Them and It was John's provocation; a book elegantly written and entertainingly delivered to answer that question. I read it and it helped me understand the power and potential of words in business.

Of course, brands use words; they have to, because you can't communicate properly without them – but you should use them well. This meant that a brand's language became integral to a brand. And, from my personal perspective, it changed the way I thought.

My perspective on business writing was transformed by John and this book. It remains a book to inspire – this time to inspire a new generation of marketers, as well as to remind those who have been around for longer that there are enduring truths in the world of marketing.

John's insistence, for example, that marketing is a creative discipline. As we slip into the lazy comfort of brand models, often twisted into unlikely graphic shapes alongside the jargon-fuelled machinations of business strategy, let's not forget that we need words. Not just any words, but words that will take us to a deeper understanding of a brand.

Although the thought still seems revolutionary to many, this might mean playing with words and stories, borrowing techniques from poetry, tapping into your inner feelings, not hiding behind the conventional formulas. The point is, it works. John showed that in the original edition, drawing on examples from his own experience, and the ideas set out then continue to resonate now.

John has, across the years, inspired many people in person. The beauty of a book like this is that it can reach a broader audience to help accelerate their understanding, and to put into action what he recommends.

This book inspired so many in the branding business, including consultants who now, as a matter of course, refer to verbal identity and tone of voice. It has inspired those who work in business (not only directly in marketing). It started here.

This is still the best business writing inspiration I've ever come across, and I'm delighted to be introducing this special edition 21 years after it was first published. It has been reprinted several times since; a sign that its relevance lives on.

After all these years, this book still has the power to provoke new thinking in the marketing and branding community. If you're reading it for the first time, I suspect it will become a critical reference source for a refreshed approach to language for you, your teams and your brands. I hope you enjoy it as much as I did when I first read it.

Sophie Devonshire
Global CEO, The Marketing Society

Preface

This book came out of an absorption in 'identity' – the word we used before 'branding' pushed it aside. Corporate identity (as it began), visual identity (as it softened), verbal identity (as I developed). Identity took people and businesses into creative areas of design with incursions across the borders into psychology. It was interesting territory, but it seemed to ignore the potential of words.

The absence of recognition for words gnawed away at me until I wrote *We, Me, Them & It* at the turn of the millennium. *"Words are your children"* was one sentence that I put in the book. Now it seems my words have grown up, perhaps coming back to haunt me. Or, from a more benign viewpoint, to remind me that I might have made a difference.

It's a strange feeling, reading your own words written by a younger version of yourself. I'd even anticipated that feeling in the original introduction. *"But almost as soon as the words are out they take on a life of their own."* That turned out to be true as the words continued to beckon me to faraway places – invitations to Memphis to talk to FedEx's team, to Zurich to help Swiss Films with their branding, to New Zealand to run a series of Dark Angels workshops.

The words in this book took me to Dark Angels. Before writing it I'd not envisaged that I would put so much of my time and enthusiasm into helping others to write more effectively. With hindsight – such a wonderful thing – I can see that *We, Me, Them & It* led inevitably to Dark Angels, an organisation that encourages 'creative writing for business'.

Originally with two colleagues, Jamie Jauncey and Stuart Delves, Dark Angels helped people weighed down by corporate writing to gain their writing wings. We took them to remote and interesting places, metaphorically and literally – to the world inside their heads, to the highlands of Scotland, a *finca* in Andalusia, a country house outside Gdansk.

There, fuelled by exercises that stretched participants creatively, they were liberated from the repressive thought – "*They* will never let me write like that". The writers – as they would now describe themselves – found that they could write with much greater imagination and freedom than they and their work organisations had believed possible, and with the confidence to stand up for this way of seeing the world.

Dark Angels grew but never aspired to become a global mega-corporation (as if!). It grew through the loyalty and evangelism of those attending courses, spreading the word, applying the principles of more humane writing. Other partners – who had all been through Dark Angels courses – swelled the number of tutors, but we were determined to remain a small group of friends and allies in words, albeit with international reach.

Still it surprised me when Neil Baker, who had become Dark Angels' managing partner, described *We, Me, Them & It* as 'the foundation text of the Dark Angels philosophy'. Had I created an academic subject or a mysterious cult? Neither, thankfully, because Dark Angels has always been grounded in the practical needs of its participants – to write, to write well and with pleasure, to write better so they could do their jobs better.

In the meantime, in the two decades of meantime that began this century, so much happened to change the environment for the use of words in business. In particular social media inserted themselves into our lives, at times bringing a bullying edge to communications, but also making inevitable the transition to a more informal style. Alongside this, politics brought in populism with big lies and fake news, changing the whole landscape for public discourse. How could we remain humane and civilised – values imbedded in this book – without losing effectiveness?

In the end it all comes down to stories. When I wrote *We, Me, Them & It*, it was unusual to use the word 'story' in a business context. Now it's become part of the everyday language that companies use. They use words to tell stories, and the best stories are authentic and illuminate the brand – which others then respond to because this leads to a better understanding of a business's reason for being. It brings us back to where it all started – to identity, and to those simple but powerful questions that drive storytelling: Who are you? Where are you from? What do you do? How do you do it? Why?

John Simmons
August 2021

Introduction

'Words don't deserve that kind of malarkey. They're innocent, neutral, precise, standing for this, describing that, meaning the other, so if you look after them you can build bridges across incomprehension and chaos.'

Tom Stoppard, *The Real Thing*

So what the hell is this book about?

I knew you would ask me that. So I must try to answer.

Let me say first what it is not. It is not a management book. Except that I believe there is a powerful connection between effective management and effective writing. But this is not a 'how to be a better manager' book.

So, I've lost a lot of sales already. I hear the sound of this book being closed in airports around the world. But who said it got in those airport bookshops in the first place? Books have to find their readers, words have to find their audiences, and there is something magically serendipitous about the process when you think about it. Written words can be read by complete strangers yet still be recognised as friends.

I might have stumbled on something there. That might be close to the theme of this book.

When we put words down on paper they come from inside our heads. But almost as soon as they are out they take on a life of their own. The writer looks at them and starts to edit them in the glare of other thoughts and other influences. My words are no longer mine, because they are shared. The meaning I intended, or even the meaning that I imagined, will not be exactly the same meaning received by you now reading these words. You will put your own interpretation on them, bringing to bear all the thoughts and experiences that have made you very different from me.

But that's all right. I'm not a control freak. Writers need readers not clones.

This book is about recognising that words are living beings. Because we are human we know that we should care about other living beings. Most of the time we do not. We let them starve through neglect. We step over them when we see them on the street trying to attract our attention. We pull the curtains so we don't have to look at them. We even lock the doors on them if we feel they threaten us.

You cannot be a writer without the ability to step outside your own personality.

At times of peace talks – Middle East, the Balkans, Ireland, wherever and whenever – I keep hearing the phrase 'people have to learn to walk in each other's moccasins'. Sadly it has become something of a cliché, causing me to suspect that it might have no meaning at all for the kind of person it is directed at.

The thought, for example, of the Reverend Ian Paisley in Gerry Adams' moccasins – in anyone's moccasins – is surreal; the thought of Ian Paisley speaking and writing in any voice other than that rasping Ulster rant is incongruous.

We all have our own personalities which shape the way we behave and the way we use words.

We might show our personalities by being effusive or mean or nervy or aggressive in our language. We are all quite comfortable with the notion that different writers have different styles. Indeed we credit the greatest writers with having the most individual and recognisable styles. We even give them their own adjectives like Dickensian or Joycean. But what really makes that style individual? Is it really a pure expression of the writer's personality?

All writing is a conversation not a monologue.

My conviction is that we all bring a number of personalities into play when we write. I am not thinking here exclusively, or even primarily, of fictional writing. My subject is writing for business, writing as a vital (some would say unavoidable) part of doing a job. My hope is to persuade you, if you need persuading, that writing should be seen positively as vital, not negatively as unavoidable. Because words are vital, they are living beings.

We me them it.

Our words are an expression of our own individual personality and that is the core of any writer's 'tone of voice' – that is **me**. But our words are also influenced by people outside ourselves. At work, the words we write are from us and from the organisation itself; friends and colleagues apply invisible pressure because we are, in a sense, writing on behalf of all of us who share part of that organisation's life. The people we write to also exert influence because you know that they will be making their own interpretation of the words they read. And the thing itself – the content of whatever it is that you have to say or write, the thing imposes its personality as well, the message influences the delivery of the message.

I express this in a simple diagram:

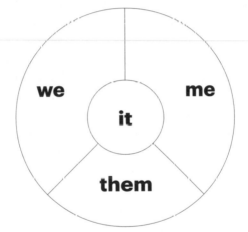

Let us focus on being a writer at work. You are employed to write **it**. It might be a letter to a customer; an annual report; a memo about organisational change; an offer of employment to someone you interviewed; a marketing idea that will make money for your company. It might be any number of things. What you are primarily concerned about is the message because it is inextricably linked to the function of the job you are paid to do.

But you can't think about it in isolation. You have to consider who else you are writing it for and who you are writing it to.

You are part of an organisation that has an identity. Whether it is conscious of it or not. That identity is shaped by the collective sense of values held by all the people working in the organisation. Each day each person offers an experience of the organisation to people outside. It can be a good or a bad experience, and clearly successful companies ensure that good experiences outnumber the bad. In this way they manage their brand. The idea of identity, closely linked to the notion of the brand, is central to the thinking in this book.

The organisation's brand represents a promise. It says: this is what we are like, this is what we want to be, and (if you wish) you can connect with us too. It follows that when you are writing as part of your job you are writing on behalf of the brand – so you need to have a clear idea what that brand stands for. You are also writing to people who will see you as brand spokesperson. The other people in your organisation will also write for the brand, but will you all be writing as if for the same brand – or will you, in effect, all be promising different things?

Of course you can't all be the same or use the same words or reduce yourselves to robotic common denominators.

Naturally you will be saying different words in different ways because you will be communicating with different kinds of people. Within an overall framework of consistent behavioural values, you should be able to adapt your words and vary your tone of voice to engage with the real needs of the person you are writing to. It is helpful to think of a person even if the reality is that you are writing to many people.

The key to doing this is not just to think of that person but also to think of your self. The trick is to bring more of *you* to your job and to your writing. You have permission to say 'I am me' – of course you do, that's why you were hired in the first place.

Liberate yourself. Bring more of your self to work. It will be better for your organisation. It will certainly be better for you.

This book is divided into four main chapters. The first chapter is about **we**. It started life some years ago as a talk I was asked to give to managers of WH Smith about the role of language in communicating a brand. At that time there was no clear idea in WH Smith about who 'we' were. Did we have a brand? If so, what did it stand for? If we have a brand, are we all part of it? As they addressed these questions, it was useful and enlightening for them to be able to move towards understanding their brand better through focusing on words and through seeing words as potentially precise instruments which shape concepts and chisel them into reality.

The second chapter is about **me**. Not necessarily in an autobiographical sense, although there is a fragment of autobiography there to make a point. The point is simply that we are all individuals and we need to express our individuality. We need to realise – for the sake of our effectiveness as well as our mental well-being – that we should pursue at work more of the individual interests and express more of the personal enthusiasms that make us what we are.

The third chapter is about **them**. They are the people and companies out there that we address words to when we are writers at work. In this part there are case studies and extracts from projects I have worked on with different clients, covering a range of businesses. The focus for these companies is: how can we communicate better with them – the customers out there whom we need for the continuing success of the business?

The fourth chapter is about **it**. It draws together ideas on the relationship between language and identity. It is about finding the distinctive content and the style to make your organisation realise more of its potential through the power of words.

Have I answered your question? If I have, or if I haven't, all I can do is ask you to read on.

1

WE THE TROUBLE WITH WORDS

'You see it's like
a portmanteau –
there are two
meanings packed
up into one word.'

Lewis Carroll, *Through the Looking-Glass*

1 Beginnings

What I want to write about first is the corporate
perspective. By this I mean writing for companies or
organisations, writing that builds or reinforces a brand,
writing that gives a clearer sense of the organisation's
identity. Writers are individuals; a company's words are
collective; we are the company. There is a tension in this
but it is a wonderful challenge to try to resolve. Which
is what we aim to do every day when we are writers
at work.

For the individual as writer the greatest problem can
be knowing how to make a beginning. We all share
the fear of the white page or the blank screen. One way
to overcome this is to carry out a conversation in your
head about the subject you are going to write about.
A conversation gets you away from being over-formal,
and normally a phrase emerges that gives a good
starting point.

Another of the things I do – rather haphazardly – is
jot down in a notebook either thoughts that occur to
me or phrases I come across and like. A little while ago I
wrote down this phrase I'd seen in a newspaper...

'The trouble with
words is you never
know whose mouths
they've been in.'

I really liked that phrase because it expressed a truth in a witty way. We are all 'green' with words – we recycle them constantly. The trick is not so much to find new words but to find new ways of saying the old words.

The truth of the phrase was also brought home to me when I first started using it because I could not remember who the hell had said it. I really wanted to know whose mouth the words had been in now that I was mouthing them too. Days passed and it was nagging away at me. Then one Sunday evening a sudden flash of remembrance struck when the TV announcer said the following...

Viewers are warned that the next programme contains explicit language

The next programme was Dennis Potter's *Lipstick on my Collar* and it is to him that I owe the title of this chapter, which I have also adapted as a running theme. The quotation I had originally noted was from an interview with Dennis Potter.

But let's just pause for a moment on this TV announcer's phrase. What it means is that some viewers might be offended by swear words. Swear words are often applied rather generally; they don't necessarily have a specific meaning. Viewers might actually prefer an explicit warning.

The trouble with words is that they don't always say what they mean.

If I'm talking to myself it doesn't particularly matter if I don't know what I'm talking about. But if I want to communicate – to get across to another person the thoughts I have in my head – then the imprecision of words starts to become a problem.

However, it's a good starting point for us all to understand that words don't necessarily communicate what we hope they will communicate. That's why I've always been interested in the combination of written and visual messages to strengthen meaning. Yet the sad truth is that in business generally, but particularly in 'brand consultancy', people either separate words from images, concentrating on visual identity, or they see words purely as tools; tools to make a frame and a canvas for a picture rather than to paint the picture itself.

*'If everybody in our company took an exam
in writing, the highest marks would go to
the 14 directors.*

*The better you write, the higher you go in
Ogilvy & Mather. People who think well,
write well.'*

When I came across this statement a couple of years ago I didn't know whether to laugh or cry. For as long as I can remember I've used writing to sort out my thinking, and to explain this to people I have said 'People who write well, think well'. And there was David Ogilvy's version in print, a good demonstration of the trouble with words, you never know whose mouth they've been in, I'd been beaten to the phrase.

Except that, in this case, I didn't mind at all. David Ogilvy, as a writer for business, was one of the great writers of the twentieth century.

David Ogilvy started life as a salesman. He wrote a guide for door-to-door salesmen on 'Selling the Aga Cooker'. It starts...

*'In Great Britain, there are twelve million
households. One million of these own
motorcars. Only ten thousand own Aga
Cookers. No household which can afford
a motorcar can afford to be without an Aga.'*

That's the start. It goes on for a dozen pages. It's brilliant. It also illustrates an important point about writing – it seems to me an inescapable principle that good writing is about selling.

I've given talks to help people write better proposals and business reports, to write better blurbs for book covers, and to write better letters. In each case the writer is trying to convince the reader to 'buy', although the exchange of money is not always essential to this buying process. The principles also apply to poetry or novel-writing. The important point is that between the buyer and the seller, the reader and the writer, a relationship needs to be built. Without that relationship there is no hope of a sale. You can call it advocacy if you like, or the argument, but it is selling in the sense that the writer is trying to persuade, convince and win someone over.

You don't always succeed. I'll be using a few examples from American politics in this book, but this one might be the only one I agree with.

'You agree with me on 9 issues out of 12, vote for me. You agree with me on 12 out of 12, go see a psychiatrist.'

Mayor Ed Koch

Perhaps the first principle of selling and writing is to seize attention. This starts with the very first words and it's a writing skill that I have long been fascinated by.

For example, for the booksellers Sherratt & Hughes we designed a series of bags which used opening lines from novels. (Sherratt & Hughes then merged with Waterstone's, and the idea was simply passed on in the merger to become an integral part of Waterstone's identity.) In selecting these lines for the bags, I was actually voting for my three favourites. The three I chose were by Joseph Heller, Jane Austen and LP Hartley. Each immediately establishes the book's tone of voice and starts to build that necessary relationship between writer and reader. It establishes that the relationship is not about 'I' but about 'we' – it takes two to communicate.

'The past is a foreign country: they do things differently there.'

From *The Go-Between* by LP Hartley

'It is a truth universally acknowledged, that a single man in possession of a good fortune, must be in want of a wife.'

From *Pride and Prejudice* by Jane Austen

'It was love at first sight.

The first time Yossarian saw the chaplain, he fell madly in love with him.'

From *Catch-22* by Joseph Heller

Tone of voice is all-important, as Keith Waterhouse pointed out in his book, originally written as the house style manual for the *Daily Mirror* in the days when it employed journalists. You can substitute the name of your company for the *Daily Mirror* and the words are still relevant.

> '...Does all this matter? Yes. Every word that appears in the *Daily Mirror*, from the splash headline to the most obscure clue in the Quizword, has a byline – the byline of the *Daily Mirror*. The pitch of the *Mirror's* voice reveals what it thinks of its readers. The voice-range runs from respect (the *Mirror* at its best) to apparent contempt (the *Mirror* at its worst).'

But let's stay with opening lines, because they offer revealing insights. This is from *Moby Dick*.

Call me Ishmael

You are immediately addressed in the most startling way. You back away but there's no escape. You're confronted with a real person.

> *'It was inevitable that the scent of*
> *bitter almonds always reminded him*
> *of the fate of unrequited love.'*
> Gabriel Garcia Marquez, *Love in the Time of Cholera*

A more subtle approach from Marquez, immediately establishing his novel's tone of regret, and through the use of key words – inevitable, bitter, fate, unrequited love – straightaway introducing the book's themes.

> *'It was the afternoon of my eightyfirst*
> *birthday, and I was in bed with*
> *my catamite when Ali announced that*
> *the archbishop had come to see me.'*
> Anthony Burgess, *Earthly Powers*

Here Anthony Burgess is really making a joke of the novelist's challenge to write a dramatic opening. How many shocking thoughts can you cram into one sentence?

One final example of opening lines from John Donne.

Sweetest love, I do not goe,
For wearinesse of thee.

—

For Godsake hold your tongue,
And let me love.

—

Busy old foole, unruly Sunne,
Why dost thou thus,
Through windowes, and through curtaines,
call on us?

Although written 400 years ago, and in verse, the easy conversational tone in each example immediately catches your interest and establishes that vital relationship between writer and reader, or perhaps more revealingly between speaker and listener. Note too the use of questions to engage you, another useful technique.

The other important point to demonstrate from looking at literature — and the way books are marketed — is that we constantly bring different interpretations to great books. Each age reinterprets a book in the light of changing history, taste, pre-occupations. This is why it's possible to read a great book again and again. In the words of Ezra Pound, on this poster we designed for Waterstone's, 'Literature is news that stays news'.

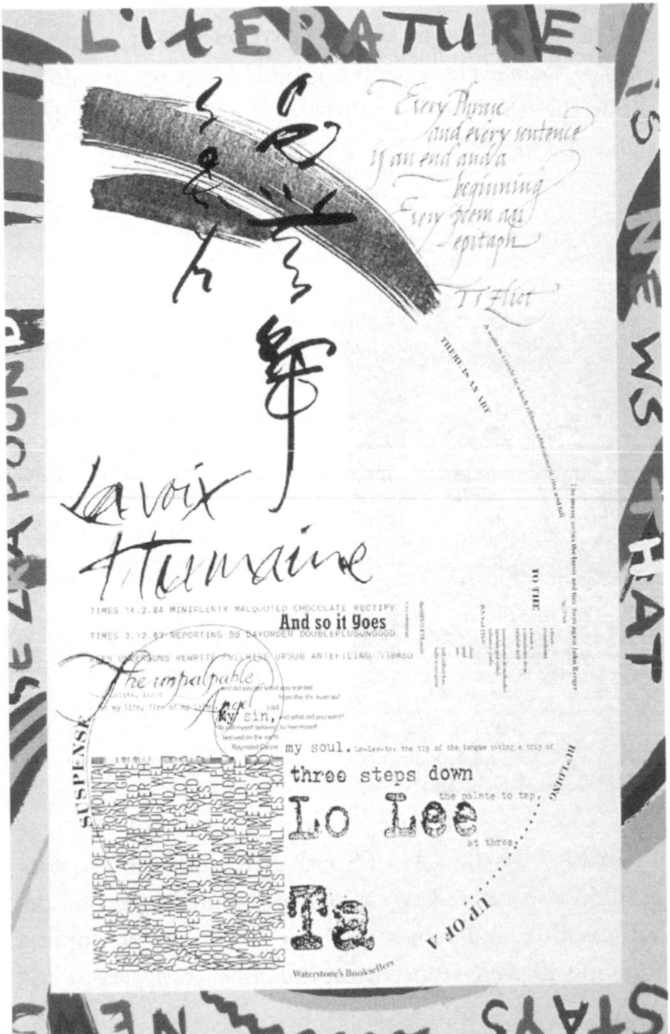
L'iterature
is news that stays news
Every Phrase
and every sentence
is an end and a
beginning
Every poem an
epitaph
T S Eliot
THERE IS AN ART
La voix Humaine
TIMES 14.2.84 MINIPLENTY MALQUOTED CHOCOLATE RECTIFY
And so it goes
TIMES 3.12.83 REPORTING BB DAYORDER DOUBLEPLUSUNGOOD
The impalpable
Angel
and did you get what you wanted
from this life, even so?
and what did you want?
beloved on the earth
Raymond Carver
my soul.
three steps down
the palate to tap,
Lo Lee
at three,
Ta
TO THE
SUSPENSE
Waterstone's Booksellers

For example, let's take these two versions of a Penguin classic, *Nostromo* by Joseph Conrad. The version below shows the front cover and part of the blurb of the edition published in 1967.

Amid the grandiose scenery of South America, against the exciting events of a revolution, Conrad ironically displays men, not as isolated beings, but as social animals.

In 1967 we thought of South America in terms of its grandiose scenery. Revolution (or the idea of revolution) was exciting, and people i.e. 'men' (although no doubt individuals) were seen within the context of society.

Below are shown the front cover and blurb of the edition published in 1990.

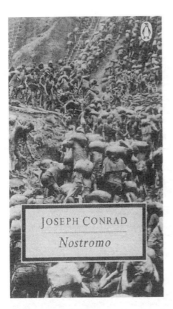

The novel captures the tragic and brutal essence of Latin-American politics as each character's potential for good is turned to corruption or defeat.

By 1990 South America is seen somewhat less romantically. Politics – closely associated with corruption – can defeat the individual and the individual's potential for good.

If we stay with Conrad, he wrote *Heart of Darkness* at the turn of the twentieth century, questioning the colonial experience in Africa in a way that no European had previously done.

By the 1970s Francis Ford Coppola had taken *Heart of Darkness* as his inspirational starting point for a film about the horror of Vietnam. Each age reassesses its own experience in its own language which reflects that experience. You need to see writing in context and that applies to any kind of writing.

2 Middles

Having established a context for my own words, let us now look at some particular points to do with language.

There is no such thing as correct use of language. Words need to do too many things for us ever to be able to say, 'Ah, that's the only one'. Of course our aim will always be to invest words with as much meaning as possible. Words, whether or not by our own deliberate intention, are always trying to break free from tight chains of meaning.

It seems to me an amazing strength of the English language that we not only give words to other languages but we take in words too.

There is almost a trade in words which adds to the richness and diversity of language. Words are sometimes ambassadors, sometimes refugees, and often they find more natural homes outside their original environment.

For example, a Hindi word **bungalow** that conjures up an essentially English way of living.

Laissez-faire a French phrase that has no English equivalent so we have adopted it as the French have taken 'Le Parking' and 'Le Weekend'. But if, on the other hand, you compare passages of English written now and in, say, 1600 the differences would be enormous compared to the changes in French over that period. English is a language in constant and relatively fast evolution, and all the richer for that.

It's also a language of inconsistency and possibilities, particularly in its spelling. The illogicality of English spelling is another sign of experimentation and invention with language. Even if we become used to it by habit, it can still be a shock to be confronted afresh by seeing just how misleading spelling can be as a guide to pronunciation. It leads people to think of alternatives.

Though	Tho
Through	Drive-thru
Plough	Plow
Rough	Ruff 'n' Tumble

For example, we all recognise 'tho' as an abbreviation of 'though'. We understand the concept of 'Drive-thru'. We might well have a feeling in the back of our mind that 'plow' is an older (or possibly American) spelling variant. And thinking about 'rough' I looked up the phone book and discovered a company called 'Ruff 'n' Tumble' which turned out to be a day nursery. George Bernard Shaw's use of 'ghoti' as part of his campaign to reform English spelling remains an interesting joke but a fish is still a fish.

The possibilities of alternative spellings indicate the potential to create new forms of language. When we think of this we think particularly of America.

Dancin' broccoli heads
Ezi-cough
Shurfine
Shoprite
Nuway

The invention of brand names such as these has been closely associated with an American way of selling and marketing.

Coca-Cola might be the most widely recognised word around the world in any language, but the *Oxford English Dictionary* would rather pretend it doesn't exist.

There are many examples in Britain too, of course.

Kwik Save
Supawash
Kar Rite
Xpert Engineering
Xtra Hair

In Britain, especially in England, there is perhaps an inherent snobbery in people's attitude towards this kind of brand name. It's hard to create an upmarket brand or a brand that stands for quality when the name depends on a misspelling. For the English it's like a social gaffe. These names mean other things to us – cheapness, lack of sophistication, a basic level of service.

INVISIBLE **EXPORT**

There is another aspect to our use of the English language. It is perhaps Britain's best asset as a nation, but it is an asset shared by other trading nations. The English language remains the greatest invisible export. It is the most international language of business and of knowledge, and it is the kind of import barrier and in-built export advantage that we imagine the Japanese would love to have invented.

It's not one that we can be complacent about, though. When Sony invented the Walkman, they were advised by their English-speaking marketing experts that the name 'Walkman' would never do. People wouldn't understand it. Instead they recommended 'Soundaround'. Fortunately Sony ignored this advice and the Walkman it was and still is.

Listen

The best advice I can give is to listen. When you write, when you use English, either say the words out loud or say them inside your head. This simple practice would kill off most examples of bad writing – and therefore of bad thinking.

'For PC3 (writing) first examine the constituent AT levels, based on the NC text levels and the TA level in the case of AT4/5. If the TA in AT4/5 (presentation) is at level 7 and the NC test level for AT3 (writing) is at level 8, then the PC level is the AT3 NC test level.

However, if the TA in AT4/5 is not at level 7, but is higher than level 4, then the PC level is worked out as follows: AT3 NC test level x8 plus AT4 TA level x2, divided by 10.'

This bad thinking, for example, comes from the UK Government's Department of Education which was attempting to get English teachers to test 14-year-olds on their English language skills. Trying to read this, our sympathies are entirely with the English teachers who decided to boycott the test.

If one civil servant (now there's an interesting job title) had read these words out to another I can't believe that they would have been printed. There is a beauty in words and we should never be ashamed to strive for that beauty.

'I put confidence in the
American people,
in their ability to sort
through what is fair
and what is unfair,
what is ugly and
what is unugly.'

George Bush

When he was US President, George Bush Senior
had a certain way with words. I found it absolutely
fascinating that Bill Clinton had three equal directors
of his 1992 Presidential election campaign team – one
responsible for strategy, one for communications, and
one (David Kusnet) for language. I like to think that the
result of the election was partly a victory for language.

Words are invested with a power beyond their size.
Let's take as a prime example the word...

David Kusnet writes about the villain for the American people always being **Big**. 'Big money, big business, and big government are all rhetorical whipping boys for populist politicians.'

> *'The story of the California environmental referendum, 'Big Green', proves the point. As some commentators observed, the ballot measure lost "not because it was green but because it was big".'*

Although I suspect that the word **green** is now also seen through a veil of cynicism. It's a word and a concept that is too easy to abuse.

In a curious echo too of his father's phrase, George W Bush was proclaimed the victor in one of the 2000 campaign primaries: 'Bush won big, but he won ugly.' Behind the sneer here, there is the hint of respect for the sheer scale of success. However, you have to say that the son has inherited much of his father's way with words. He was quoted as saying the following during his campaign:

> *'When I was coming up, it was a dangerous world and we knew exactly who they were. It was us versus them, and it was clear who them was. Today, we're not so sure who the they are. But we know they're there.'*

The trouble with words is that they have a life of their own.

There is a cultural difference there between the US and the UK. I think the UK is less sensitive to the issues surrounding 'Big' and perhaps the image of James Stewart going to Washington is less mythic for the British public.

But David Kusnet goes on to make an observation which we can apply to the communication style of any country, and this lesson is certainly not confined to politics nor to the English language alone.

His observation was about the 1988 US election, when in a scripted speech George Bush talked about his yearning for

A kinder, gentler America

The words are words that you would use to describe a real person. That is their strength, that's what gives them life.

They place an image before everyone who hears them that can be individually adapted to fit that person's experience. By contrast, Dukakis' speechwriters, trying to say the same sort of thing, talked about 'a more decent, compassionate society'. It sounded benevolent but bureaucratic.

I invite you to apply the same analysis to your own companies. I've hardly mentioned businesses or companies up to this point, and that has been deliberate. I get excited by words and I get depressed by uniformity. I hate the way that companies exclude the animate from their language. There is, for example, a whole language of 'personnel' which denies the humanity which has to be at the heart of that particular function. 'Human resources' is a symptom of this kind of thinking.

A kinder, gentler Ford Motor Company
A kinder, gentler Post Office
A kinder, gentler IBM

and so on...

Words can move, explain, startle, excite, persuade, express ideas... and more.

These words are words I use to express my own beliefs. I enjoy writing and I would love everyone else to enjoy it too. If you learn to love words you will automatically learn to write better.

3 Ends

For the final section of this chapter, I need to narrow the focus to the use of language and corporate or brand identity.

Let me start with an example of the emotional power of words within a company's identity. The example is the United States Post Office building in New York. There is an inscription that runs across the building and which reads:

> 'Neither snow nor rain nor heat nor gloom
> of night stays these couriers from the swift
> completion of their appointed rounds.'

Now there is something that strikes us as quaint and old-fashioned in that. It almost needs Cliff Claven, the white-socked mail man from *Cheers*, to stand, hand on heart, and declaim it. But despite that it seems to me a beautiful, ringing and distinctive statement of the value of public duty. I would argue against any cynicism – the statement remains a wonderful vision of public service, a statement that expresses and engenders pride. A statement that implies 'we have a common cause in working for this organisation'.

A lot of organisations try to achieve a similar effect with Latin mottos. Most of these have a genuine traditionalism which makes them acceptable.

PER ARDUA AD ASTRA
VICTORIA CONCORDIA CRESCIT
NIL SATIS NISI OPTIMUM

I doubt, however, whether we would identify strongly with a new company which tried to import a spurious tradition through the use of a Latin motto. We might think of it as a 'nouveau riche' company at best, rather dodgy at worst.

Sometimes, though, you can reverse expectations. Lumino was a new name and identity for a company that was previously called HWS Contracts. HWS were the initials of the owner's name. When his sons came into the business, instead of installing electrical ring mains, they wanted to sell sophisticated Italian lighting to architects. But, of course, they couldn't do that while they were called HWS Contracts.

The name Lumino sounded right for an Italian lighting supplier. But it was an invented name, drawing on the Latin word 'Lumen' for light. If we went back that far, could we not go further? So Lumino – as my story went – was the name of the beautiful youth who was loved by Selene the Goddess of the Moon in classical mythology. Unrequited love, unfortunately, because Lumino rejected the Goddess's advances again and again, while he tended his sheep at night on the lower slopes of Mount Olympus. At last Selene could take no more rebuffs – in a fit of anger she struck Lumino dead with a shaft of divine light. No sooner was the deed done than remorse overcame the Goddess. She pleaded with Zeus, who was touched by her story; Zeus made Lumino immortal by turning him into a star, one of the brightest in the night sky.

Pure invention, of course, but the story was completely swallowed by the design and architectural press and Lumino as a company got the best possible marketing launch.

Some companies have deliberately used a style of language that is unexpectedly partisan. The Body Shop has a distinctive visual style that we all recognise. But what I think drives that style is the company's campaigning stance which carries through everything it does. By proclaiming 'Trade not Aid' it sets a style of language, which demands a matching visual style, and it appeals to the social consciences of its customers to give them a different and distinctive reason for buying Body Shop products. And there is no doubt that it attracts people to work in the company who wish to embrace The Body Shop's principles. Again language makes identification easier.

WHY WE ARE DIFFERENT:

WE RESPECT THE ENVIRONMENT
Reuse – Refill – Recycle

WE ARE AGAINST ANIMAL TESTING FOR COSMETICS
Cruel – Unnecessary – Misleading

WE HAVE A NON–EXPLOITATIVE APPROACH TO TRADE
Equality – Employment – Trade not Aid

WE MEET THE REAL NEEDS OF REAL PEOPLE
No Idealised Images – No Extravagant Claims

WE CAMPAIGN FOR ISSUES WE BELIEVE IN

Sometimes, though, you are struggling to make fairly clichéd ideas seem different. Not every company can be cutting edge and the people working in those companies need the reassurance of the relatively familiar. They say, in effect, 'we only joined to do a job, not to change the world' – but they still need to feel pride in a job well done.

GOOD OLD-FASHIONED SERVICE

Brought to you by modern technology with a human face

Everyone now talks about customer service. For ITPS, the book distribution business of International Thomson, we created a visual and written approach that acknowledged the fact that everyone is now talking about customer service. Through the approach we took we were saying, often in so many words, that customer service is not a new notion to ITPS.

A lot of the work I did with the publisher Routledge on their identity was to do with the use of language. We started by defining the company as inquisitive, questioning, keen to explore the byways as well as the highways of academic publishing. This led to a copy style that reflected this questioning approach, and which had the parallel aim of making Routledge books more accessible to booksellers and book buyers. By using the device of two questions to lead into a back cover blurb, I was able to encourage people at Routledge to demonstrate this inquisitive nature. The language template became a literal demonstration of 'what we are about'.

What is it like
being a man
today?

Has feminism had
any real impact on
men's lives?

For many companies, clarity of communication should be part of the brand. In a busy railway station or airport, or in the streets of our towns, clear and informative signing is a customer service. Sometimes this kind of helpfulness can go astray. This was the sign in the manufacturing company's lift we entered on our way to a meeting.

When we began working with the train company InterCity our observation was that the InterCity visual language at the stations was the same as that used for directing people to the toilets. If the visual language needed to change, so too did the written language. It started with a simple statement of mission.

> *'InterCity is, quite simply, the most civilised way to travel at speed from city centre to city centre.'*

I particularly liked the use of the word *civilised*. With mission statements there is a seemingly irresistible temptation to use portmanteau words like 'best', 'quality', 'excellence'. Here was a different, surprising, but still aspirational word. And again, like the US Post Office, it contained an idea of public service that suggested deep roots.

The InterCity copywriting guidelines followed the principle 'Less is more'. These are principles to abide by, not rules to follow. The only rule is for people always to think about the language they are using.

'Good writing should aim to inform. It does this by being simple, clear and logical. Sometimes it needs to do more. It has to excite and stimulate.

Bad writing does none of these things. It confuses, frustrates and irritates the reader.

It is easier to write badly than to write well. The essence of InterCity is to do things well.'

THE POWER TO DELIVER

Sometimes language – or a phrase – is used as a deliberate and identifiable basic element of an identity system. For Parcelforce our phrase was *The Power to Deliver* which I am happy to call a slogan, for a slogan originally meant a war cry. Parcelforce needed an aggressive and confident statement as part of an identity that would help them to compete more aggressively in their market against companies like TNT, FedEx and UPS. But as part of the British Post Office – Royal Mail Parcels – they had kept a very low profile, despite being the biggest player in the market. At least the slogan lifted a few heads and puffed out a few chests inside the company – it had a resonance with the internal as well as the external audience.

ROB1NSON
CARE COMES FIRST

By contrast, our work for Robinson led to a much gentler, more caring phrase as part of this company's identity. Around for over 150 years, Robinson manufactures products for healthcare and packaging. *Care comes first* was used to express a quality commitment to people who worked for Robinson. It was also linked with the numeral 1 from the company logotype.

Other companies have other phrases. Some of them, through consistent repetition over many years, achieve instant recognition and identification with the company or brand. You will almost certainly know the companies behind these phrases.

We try harder

Never knowingly undersold

The world's favourite airline

Everything we do is driven by you

Think different

And it's more than probable that you will associate a brand of beer with this single word.

This is probably the great triumph of twentieth-century English copywriting – to invest a brand with qualities of excellence through the use of a single word, and a word that seems to claim nothing.

The trouble with words is... that they can run away with you.

We try very hard to control words but sometimes they do get out of control. Words are your children. Be aware of them, don't let them run riot while you pretend that they have nothing to do with you. They can inflict small, unthinking acts of cruelty on your neighbours.

'We have a problem of biological leakage.'

This was said by the marketing director of the *Daily Telegraph* a few years ago. It referred to the problem of older readers dying off. I suggest that this is not the kind of language to use when thinking about any group of customers. It dehumanises them and stops you thinking about them as people – it also dehumanises all of us who work for that company, because we all share the problem of biological leakage.

'I don't mind the prospect of growing old. Particularly when I think about the alternative.'

Dave Allen

To take a serious point from a good joke, think about the alternative. In language, there always is an alternative. Avoid the hackneyed ways of saying things and try to produce words that seem freshly delivered.

Think about the words you use. I've talked about first words and arresting openings. Remember that you also need a good middle and a good end. A good end might be what Dave Allen meant by the alternative. But make sure you get to your conclusion and some memorable last words. Unlike General Sedgwick who raised his head above the parapet at the Battle of the Wilderness and said...

Nonsense! They

couldn't hit an elephant at this d

SOMETHING INSIDE 2 ME

'The places where water comes together with other water. Those places stand out in my mind like holy places.'

Raymond Carver

1 Finding your voice

The first chapter looked at writing from the perspective of **we** (the corporate viewpoint), this chapter looks at writing from the perspective of **me** (the personal viewpoint). I don't think the two are, or should be, easily divisible. We need to develop a more personal writing style within the overall framework of the tone of voice of the organisation we work for.

We all have our own voice. There is something in the DNA of our voice that makes it unique and recognisable. When we use the telephone we don't always feel the need to identify ourselves by announcing our name – the voice itself is identification enough.

So too with the written word, although here it is harder to be individual. There is a distinctiveness that we value in the written voice of a great writer, but there have been few writers who have achieved such distinctiveness. Most of us have to be content with writing as well as we can, communicating what we mean as effectively as possible, and introducing occasional phrases that have the ring of our own individuality. But we need to realise too that in a world populated by billions of people the concept of individuality is a relative one.

We are all part of a linguistic river that is much greater than the little tributary we each represent. So, although we each have our individual idiosyncrasies of linguistic expression, we often do not realise that this individuality comes from a collective source. Seamus Heaney is fascinating in his description of finding the Anglo-Saxon poem *Beowulf* to be part of what he called his 'voice-right'. It was only when he came to realise this, through making the link between the Old English word 'tholian' and an Irish dialect word from his childhood 'thole' (suffer), that he could find the right tone of voice to translate the poem into a modern version. The tone was that of 'big-voiced scullions', the voice of his own Irish family members, 'a kind of Native American solemnity of utterance, as if they were announcing verdicts rather than making small talk'.

We can each, therefore, draw our individual tone of voice from what enters our personal consciousness from family, national, local, religious, historical, social, corporate and other sources. This does not diminish our individuality, it enriches it as long as we feel enabled to use all the sources to inform our individual tone of voice – as long as we do not allow one source to dominate at the expense of any other source. This is why so much writing for business is bad. People allow the corporate source to overwhelm all the other sources which should be used to create writing which is rich and compelling.

This chapter of the book is about 'giving permission' to be more personal in business writing – simply because such a style will be better for business by engaging better with people (just think who you are writing for). This chapter is also about finding ways to do that. The ways suggested here, particularly the use of poetry, have worked for me. Others might find other ways. We are all subject to different interests, susceptible to different stimuli.

2 Talking to Oxfam

This section contains a talk I gave when introducing a
workshop. The workshop was for 16 writers in Oxfam.
In 1999 Interbrand Newell and Sorrell created a new
visual identity for Oxfam, based on developing an
understanding of what this 'brand' truly stands for as
well as how we should recognise it by its visual style and
symbols. My role in this was to help Oxfam in the UK
to develop its tone of voice consistently and to express
the values of the brand through the written work
produced by the communications team in Oxford. We
brought the 16 people together in a one-day workshop
run by myself and my writing colleague Mark Griffiths.

From discussions before the workshop it emerged
that the 16 people might feel a little threatened by this
process. They were all counted as writers, but they had
different degrees of confidence in their writing ability.
They all worked for this non-profit organisation and
they didn't want to be 'commercialised'. Would we try
to turn them into charity versions of Ronald McDonald?
Would we try to get them to sell their souls through
the introduction of 'adspeak' (which, to this audience,
meant 'at the expense of honesty')?

Of course, the answer to these questions was 'no' but
I had some sympathy with the questions. I didn't know
if we would be able to help. In the event the workshop
did help those taking part – largely by boosting their
self-confidence – and it reinforced my belief in the need
for any organisation to encourage greater self-expression
at work if it is to achieve its corporate objectives
more effectively. Perhaps, looking back at the history

of the last century, we can apply the same lessons to business life as we hope we have applied to political life: totalitarianism does not work.

This is the talk that introduced the workshop.

Start of talk

It's a rare treat for Mark and myself to be in a room full of writers. In fact there's almost a contradiction in the concept because writers are generally, by their nature, happier when they have a room to themselves. Writing's a solitary business most of the time. I'm happy with that, indeed I'm happy to celebrate that, but today's about writers getting together, sharing thoughts and ideas, and working together.

Mark and I are writers. We work with companies on tone of voice issues. That means we're concerned with the way that language is used to express a company's identity. People are much more used to thinking of identity as a visual issue – it's about logotypes, symbols, colours and so on. We're interested in the relationship between brands and language. After all, we judge organisations by the way they communicate with us – using words and images together.

My understanding is that at Oxfam you work in teams which bring writers and designers together. You know that images can stimulate words, and words can suggest images. What came first in the Christian Aid advert about third world debt? Was it the picture in someone's mind of politicians stripped to their underpants – or was it the phrase 'all mouth and no trousers'?

There's a further point in this. I really believe we can and should bring our real selves to work. The things that we find interesting, intriguing and amusing are what make us the writers that we are. Our personalities inform our writing. If we're talking about writing 'on-brand' we want to write in the personality of the brand – but the reality is that the brand will only have personality if you put some of your own personalities into it.

So I decided that this intro talk should be about some things that interest me and that make me a writer. I hope it won't be as egocentric as that might sound because there's one thing we share as writers – and that's a fascination with words. Here are some words that have made an impact on my life recently, some episodes in my life, like episodes in *Frasier*.

'CAN YOU PULL IN OVER THERE AND DEBARK'

This was said to me when I arrived for a meeting near Canary Wharf. Give a man a uniform and does he have to become officious? And does he then feel the need to talk in a way that he would never do when talking with his friends? The fact is I was really quite grateful to him because his awful invention of the word 'debark' – and isn't it strange how we all know what he meant by it? – that invention gave me the idea of using these episodes today.

WENGER CAN'T SPEND HIS WONGA

WENGER CAN'T SPEND HIS WONGA

Perhaps the only surprise, if you knew me a little, might be that a reference to my football team, the Arsenal, was so long delayed. This was a headline in *The Sun* one summer as the close season drew to an end and still Arsenal had signed no new players. You can rely on *The Sun* for an arresting headline and I enjoy it for the headlines, but I worry that it's another of those signs that we're all turning into being simply readers of headlines.

I love football for its passion – something we'll talk about more – and simply because, a lot of the time, it makes me feel good.

OH AMERICAAH!

I'm fascinated by America. Sometimes it can be amazingly expansive with its language, particularly with place names. The Admiral Pulatski Skyway seems to me a beautiful name for what might have been called Pulatski Bridge.

But as I was travelling to a meeting down the New Jersey Turnpike – another expansive name – I came across the opposite tendency. Sometimes American expansiveness gives way to US contraction. Sitting in the back of a limo I saw this sign by the side of the road.

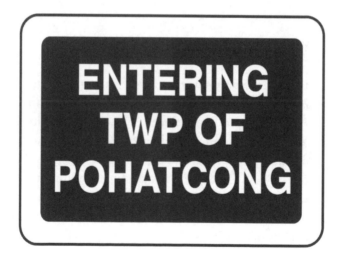

Now I always loved cowboys and indians, so I got a flutter of interest that this might be a Native American historical site. I wondered how to pronounce it – Twop, perhaps, or Tope or Toop. But then a few miles down the road this sign was followed by Twp of Bridgewater, Twp of Bedminster and a township dawned on me.

It reminded me of this lovely contraction in San Francisco – nothing to do with Chinatown, simply a matter of crossing the road and watching out for cable cars.

'JUST PICKED UP A LOT OF POBS'

This was a few days later, returning from America and making my way at Heathrow back to my parked car. What happens is you get on the bus to collect your car from the Business Car Park.

As I sat down I overheard the driver speaking on his radio – 'Just picked up a lot of POBs. Alright to come back?' I guess that means Passengers on Board – but perhaps it's worse. It also occurs to me that the title Courtesy Bus might be ironic.

WHAT'S IN A NAME?

One of the interesting things over the last year
has been to observe some of the uses of names in
everyday use. There's been a lot of talk of Draconian
laws, and we all know what draconian means but
perhaps we know very little about the ancient Greek
called Draco. Should we know more? Perhaps in
his day people made fun of his name – perhaps he
locked people up for doing so. And then, of course,
there was Bill Clinton's continuing troubles and the
passing into the language – for how long, I wonder
– of the term 'the full Monica'. Of course, we've got
rid of these political scandals in the UK haven't we? I
thought so but then I was shocked by this headline in
the *Daily Telegraph*.

Cabinet pay to be squeezed for three years

RHAPSODY IN WOODY

I can't help it. Despite everything, I still love Woody
Allen's films. I love them less and less for Woody's
own performances but more and more for the quality
of his writing. Having got back from America,
having seen the Manhattan skyline in the distance
but not, this time, having the chance to go there –
I bought the video of one of my favourite Woody
Allen films *Manhattan*, and I'll now play you the
opening couple of minutes.

*The opening of Manhattan is a sequence of black and white
images of New York, with George Gershwin's Rhapsody
in Blue heard over the scenery of skyscrapers, parking lots,
bridges, neon lights, Central Park and so on. You hear
Woody Allen's voice speaking over the imagery, playing
the part of the novelist struggling to write the opening lines
of a book about New York. He tries and discards many
different approaches: the romanticised, the street-smart, the
preachy, the angry. The images change to reflect the direction
set by the words before finally he resolves the problem of the
opening lines by writing the words that reflect his best image
of himself. 'Behind his black-rimmed glasses was the coiled
sexual power of a jungle cat.' The Gershwin music rises
to a crescendo, while images of fireworks explode over the
Manhattan skyline.*

PHWOAH

A few months ago Oxford University Press came out
with a new version of the *Oxford English Dictionary*.

It seemed to create quite a stir. This always seems an easy way for newspapers to manufacture a bit of controversy. Look what new words have officially now entered the English language, given credibility by appearing in the dictionary. Well, there's *Phwoah* defined as 'appreciation of the opposite sex by the inarticulate'.

CONVERSATIONS WITH MY AGENT

No, I don't have one, my royalties are too small. This is about my trip to Edinburgh, for the first time to the Festival. One of the performances I was keen to see was the theatrical adaptation of Rob Long's book *Conversations with my Agent*. Rob Long had been one of the writers of *Cheers*, one of my favourite TV programmes.

There's one funny piece where Rob Long, following the end of *Cheers*, was getting ever more desperate to find producers for some of his new writing for a new sitcom. He tells a story as a moral dilemma, to show his plight as a writer. It goes like this:

A writer friend of mine offers this moral puzzler. You are travelling in the Brazilian rainforest. You come across an ageing, though still spry, Adolf Hitler. You tell him that he is the greatest villain of the twentieth century and that it will give you great pleasure to turn him in to the authorities. He tells you that he's seen your show and he thinks it is 'wunderbar'. Do you turn him in?

For a writer it can be terrible – when people pass judgement on your words they pass judgement on you. It's impossible not to take it personally and, God knows, I've had enough practice by now. So I guess all I'm saying is – I understand how you can feel vulnerable as writers. Today's not going to be about making judgements or critiques, it's about exploring together a subject that we all love.

TREAD SOFTLY BECAUSE YOU TREAD ON MY DREAMS

This is the last line of a poem by Yeats. It gave me an idea that has led to some of the more magical moments of my working life. Over the last year, with 35 brave volunteers from Interbrand Newell and Sorrell, we've been conducting an experiment with poetry. I've selected poems for each of those 35 people and they've lived with those poems for a period of weeks, getting deeper into their meaning day by day before giving me a written response. What did the poem mean to them? Could they bring some of that emotional meaning into their working life?

The responses have been extraordinary. It has been emotional. It's confirmed my belief that people are amazing, that people can bring more of themselves to work. And, if they do, it's nothing but positive.

Mark Griffiths paid me back in kind by choosing a poem for me. It's called *What is the word*. And it's by Samuel Beckett.

> *folly —*
> *folly for to —*
> *for to —*
> *what is the word —*
> *folly from this —*
> *all this —*
> *folly from all this —*
> *given —*
> *folly given all this —*
> *seeing —*
> *folly seeing all this —*
> *this —*
> *what is the word —*
> *this this —*
> *this this here —*
> *all this this here —*
> *folly given all this —*
> *seeing —*
> *folly seeing all this this here —*
> *for to —*
> *what is the word —*
> *see —*
> *glimpse —*
> *seem to glimpse —*
> *need to seem to glimpse —*
> *folly for to need to seem to glimpse —*
> *what —*
> *what is the word —*

and where –
folly for to need to seem to glimpse what
where –
where –
what is the word –
there –
over there –
away over there –
afar –
afar away over there –
afaint –
afaint afar away over there what –
what –
what is the word –
seeing all this –
all this this –
all this this here –
folly for to see what –
glimpse –
seem to glimpse –
need to seem to glimpse –
afaint afar away over there what –
folly for to need to seem to glimpse afaint
    afar away over there what –
what –
what is the word –

what is the word

Mark wanted my response to explain something of my creative approach to writing. I would say this. Writing is a desperate and sometimes a very lonely search for something that might not actually be attainable. Perfection is always within sight but always out of reach. But you keep trying and sometimes you seem to get closer to reaching that place that's in your mind. Along the way you have little triumphs. You seem to find the right word, or at least a word that seems better than the one you had used before. And in the end, it's not as bleak as the Beckett can seem and I think there is in Beckett a terrible, awe-inspiring struggle towards some kind of joy that goes simply with the process of going on.

Going on's what I've been doing for long enough now. We should get on with our workshop.

End of talk

3 Begin at home

People join charities like Oxfam because they want to express their personal beliefs through the work they do. They make sacrifices in terms of salary to gain a greater sense of satisfaction from doing a job that does some good.

But, even if we don't work for a charity, we all like to feel that we are doing good at work. Perhaps this good is simply contributing to the economic and social well-being of the place where we work (and, therefore, of the people we work with).

We all need to feel that we are remaining reasonably true to our own nature and beliefs in the work we are doing. There is acute discomfort in the notion that we are different people inside and outside work. If that notion is pushed too hard by the employer, it is time to put greater distance between yourself and your work by leaving it. Sensible employers, however, realise that there is a connection between effectiveness and happiness at work.

We need to ask, though: What makes us happy? We also need to ask: What makes each of us good at our job? I have always found that the way to get the best out of me at work is to enable me to be more myself. Don't make me do things I'm no good at. Don't force me to do things against my beliefs. *Do* encourage me to develop my real personal interests because that will also benefit the business. This might sound excessively self-centred but in fact it's not about me me me. In building and running teams I have followed these same principles and I find it works for others and for the business itself.

Of course, this means we all need a belief and confidence in what we are as individual human beings. You have to feel comfortable with yourself. You have to feel that there is value in what you are as a human being. Some people have this self-confidence naturally; for others self-confidence can just be a façade.

For myself, I have never been outwardly brimming with self-confidence but deep down I have always had personal conviction. I suspect many others are similar. What follows is something very personal, but it might also recommend to others a way of building personal conviction and developing self-expression through a particular kind of writing. I also think it's vital for me to demonstrate some of what I have been writing. You need to know more about me so that you can understand more of the different sources that contribute to my tone of voice.

The piece that follows was written a few years ago as a letter to my children (then in their late teens). Because of events in my personal life (relatives and friends suffering illness) I felt a need to put down on paper some thoughts and facts about my life so that my children could read them. I could have spoken these things to them – but I would have done so incompletely and awkwardly. Matthew and Jessie read the letter and told me that they appreciated it. I was pleased to have done it as a kind of therapy – and also because I believe it helped me in bringing more emotion, when needed, to my writing at work.

Start of letter

Dear Matthew and Jessie

On Christmas Day I went out for my run first thing. I set out in darkness and gradually it became light. I ran through Highgate Woods and as I ran I thought 'I've seen the light of another day'. It seemed to me that those words could be the first or last line of a poem about mortality and growing older.

I'm afraid I do think about mortality now, it just comes naturally with age. Mike being ill adds to the feeling; then there's Ce who's alive in her body but not in her mind; and Geoff wanting to extend the idea of storytelling therapy based on his memoir of Arnold, his dad. The fact is I really liked Geoff's little book about Arnold, and I do think it's a lovely idea.

So all these things came together and I decided to try and write down something for you about my family. About Ce in particular because it's important to try to remember her, not as she is now with all memory wrung out but as she used to be, and as you might still recognise her from your own memories. And about my mum and dad as well, Jessie and Frank, whom you never met, which is perhaps the saddest thing in my life.

★ ★ ★

I grew up in Levita House between King's Cross and Euston stations. We had a two-bedroomed flat on the third floor of a between-wars Council-owned block. I shared one bedroom with my brother Dave who was nine years older than me so we never had a lot in common. Dave had been born in 1939 just before the war broke out, and spent much of the war evacuated to Wales. Then I came along three years after the war ended and I had the childhood that poor Dave never had the chance to enjoy. By the time I started to be aware of things, I knew that there was no war (although it was still close enough to cast a shadow of fear), and I could have all sorts of things (sweet rationing was over) and, as a family, we had holidays at the seaside. Above all, I had my mum and dad with me, which Dave hadn't had until he was six.

Dave and I used to fight a bit. It shames me to say we never got on all that well; and when Dave died so young (aged 41) I felt full of guilt and remorse and regrets for things left unsaid between us. Because we did love each other but never said so because we never understood each other.

The only person who did understand Dave, at least in his last ten years, was Ce, my mum's sister. After mum and dad died – and to some extent before that too – Ce was Dave's mum, and mine too. Why was this? Partly because she was there and mum now wasn't. Partly because Jessie, my mum, and Ce were incredibly alike and close to each other all through their lives. Ce just carried on when Jessie wasn't there any more. It always amazed me that they shared a birthday, October 26th, although two years separated their births. That had to mean something.

When Dave died, it was Ce who rang me that Saturday evening to give me the news. Dave had collapsed in the gardens near Euston Station and died of a heart attack. He'd spent the day at a union meeting and given a speech in favour of the amalgamation of his smaller union with a bigger one. In a way it went against everything he'd tried to do in his working life, it was an acceptance of defeat, and he must have been under great stress. He was on his own when he died, and he'd been on his own most of the time when he was alive, but it was Ce's name and number they found on him and it was Ce that they rang to identify the body.

★ ★ ★

I hadn't meant this to be so gloomy. It's just come out that way. Let me try and tell you more about Jessie, Frank, Ce and Les. I always said – and I meant it – that Jessie was my best friend. She had a great gift for making and keeping friends. I've still never met anyone so full of life, although I can think of another Jessie who has many of the same qualities.

You have to remember that this was another age. Jessie was born in 1912. Her dad was killed in the Great War, so she never knew him. Her mum, another Jessie, brought up her and Ce all by herself, working as an early-morning cleaner. When Jessie grew up she wasn't going to have any of that. Without bitterness she knew that she'd had a raw deal, but so had millions of others. She was going to make sure her kids had a better deal.

First, there was politics. For my mum, politics were all about changing the world for the better. She wasn't a political philosopher, she was just a doer. I grew up surrounded by her political activism. She was part of the rent strike in St Pancras, one of the earliest memories I have of political action and demonstrations. From the earliest years we would go on marches (every May Day and the CND marches from Aldermaston to London at Easter).

In the 1930s she'd been a Communist. So had Frank, my dad, although his political belief never ran as deep as my mum's. In the time of the Spanish Civil War, when just married, they'd fostered a Spanish boy called Jesus. He went back to his family in Bilbao when the war was over, and in gratitude they'd made and sent us the desk which was first used by Dave and is now Matthew's.

I always loved the story about the Jarrow March.

The unemployed people of Jarrow near Newcastle marched to London in the 1930s to draw attention to the poverty caused by government policies. Jessie was outraged and moved when she went along to Hyde Park to clap the weary, ragged marchers. She didn't ask Frank, she just took along the suit he was going to wear for the wedding and she gave it to the marchers. One of those poor, hungry men must have returned to Jarrow strangely well-dressed but still poor and hungry.

All this 'Communist' activity meant that when the war started the Special Branch raided Frank and Jessie's home. I'd love to be able to ask them more about that but of course I can't. I expect the Special Branch confiscated a copy of *The Ragged-Trousered Philanthropists*.

There were always good, funny stories about clothes. Jessie loved clothes, especially hats. There was this woman, Little Edie, who lived in the next block and I used to go with my mum once a month to her flat so that Jessie could choose a new hat to buy. They were very cheap because no doubt the hats were all knocked off. But it hardly seemed criminal, more a matter of redistribution of wealth...

There was the story of the demob suits (when soldiers were discharged at the end of the war, they were each given a 'civilian' suit to return home in place of the uniform). The demob suits, which I never saw, always brought tears of laughter when Jessie and Ce remembered Frank and Les in them (they didn't fit). And then there were the swimming costumes. Frank and Les came out of the army together (same tank regiment) and everyone had a job or got a job in printing. I can't remember who was working on

the *News Chronicle* but I think it was Ce. Anyway she
got three *News Chronicle* swimsuits for Frank, Les and
Harry Sutton (my uncle, married to Trudy, Frank's
sister). The swimsuits were an early example of 'own
branding' with the paper's name sewn into the front
of these one piece woollen outfits. Les was very slim
at this time and the combination of his physique,
an oversize swimsuit and sodden wool led to one of
those images that you can see in your mind although
no photograph exists.

One of my earliest memories is going with Frank
after Nursery School to the Festival of Britain (in
1951). It's the first time I can remember playing and
it's probably because it was the only place (although
temporary) to have real equipment for children to
play on. Otherwise it was the bombed sites.

I used to enjoy it on Fridays when Frank picked me
up after school. We'd walk through Covent Garden
market, from my school in Drury Lane. Frank's
dad and Jessie's dad had both worked in Covent
Garden as porters, so there was a family interest in
the market. Sometimes Frank would take me to the
pictures in Charing Cross Road – I can remember
seeing the *Three Stooges*.

Frank collected me on Fridays because he worked
four nights a week from Monday to Thursday. He'd
leave for work at about six in the evening and get
home about twelve or thirteen hours later. This
meant that for most of the weekday evenings there

was just me and my mum at home. Jessie would bring home all the newspapers – she got them free because she always worked in the papers – and she'd read them all. Although surrounded by all this reading I never seemed to take to it. It's a mystery to me still. It was only when a teacher at school read *The Wind in the Willows* out loud in class every day that I thought there might be something in this reading lark. I told Jessie. She bought me *The Wind in the Willows* for my ninth birthday. She wrote in it, we've still got it. It was the first book I ever read. After that reading became an obsession. I loved the *Biggles* books, *Just William* and *Jennings*.

The weekends were different because mum and dad were both around at the same time. Saturdays were divided into three parts. The first part (morning) I went shopping with my mum. Up and down Chalton Street getting the groceries. Because Jessie worked in the week (still not the norm in those days) we had more shopping to do on Saturdays than other families where the mother didn't go to work. We went to the Co-op (divi number 1257861) and other shops like Fred Fields, the hardware store (I remember the smell of vinegar he used to sell from barrels – you took your own bottle for him to fill). Loaded up with shopping bags, Jessie and I would return home for her to cook lunch – something like a meat pie or stew – before Saturday moved onto part two (afternoon).

Ah yes, you've guessed, this was dad taking me to the Arsenal. We'd walk for ten minutes, often with Dave too, down the road to King's Cross. It got more exciting with every step because more and more people started heading the same way with the same purpose and it was wonderful to feel part of this same mission. At King's Cross we all headed down into the tube and by now everyone was talking and it was jolly. At Arsenal tube it started to get a bit more tense, not because of trouble but because the match was now closer. The memory is still vivid of walking up the slope of Arsenal tube, the excitement of it, holding my dad's hand, with that strange fenced-off walkway on the right where occasional passengers slipped down to get on a tube, going against the flow, while we, among the great throng, headed onward and upward to Highbury. And then into the daylight, and into Highbury. Inside, on the North Bank, Frank would meet his mates two barriers back behind the goal. They seemed very old to me, and I suppose they were men in their forties, but everyone looked older at that time. But it's true that football then wasn't so much a young man's sport. I'd sit on a cushion on the barrier, or a year or two later stand on the fold-up stool that Frank had made just for this purpose. I'd listen to the Arsenal stories of Bastin and Drake, Male and Hapgood, Alex James and Jimmy Logie, and I formed my first hero-worshipping passion for Derek Tapscott, our number 8 – just like Ian Wright.

Funnily enough I think I didn't really enjoy the matches all that much. I was always too nervous for enjoyment in the normal sense. I used to long for and dread the match. I hated losing and we lost a lot in those days. But I could never stop going and I was amazed when, in the 1960s, Frank decided he'd had enough of going to the Arsenal. By then I could go by myself and I didn't need a stool to stand on.

Saturday evenings (part three of the day) were relaxation after the match. I'd be sent down to the sweet shop to buy chocolates and sweets so we could all settle down and watch telly. The television was black and white, of course, and probably the screen was about twelve inches wide. There were terrible programmes like *Billy Cotton's Bandshow, Saturday Night Out* and *Armchair Theatre*. Saturday night television was even worse than today (no *Match of the Day*). I suspect that Frank thought that television was this bad every night, so he minded having to work at night a bit less.

Sundays were different again. In those days, there was a real sense that Sunday had to be treated as something special. People would dress up in suits. I even had to wear a tie and (short-trousered) suit if we were going out. The tie was on a bit of elastic that slipped under the shirt collar. On the streets people strolled in family groups, but everyone was quiet. The noise level fell dramatically on Sunday. Even the kids played quietly.

Around about 1958, when I was 10, we got our first car. Frank had driven tanks in the war, and he was a very careful, good driver. He loved his first car (a Hillman) and the ones that followed it, and he joined in the Sunday morning pastime of wash-the-car. In the late morning we would drive to Ce and Les's to have Sunday dinner there. Jo had been born in 1954 and I really enjoyed having her to play with. Les would generally cook lunch because Ce was never one to go along with stereotyped views of what male and female roles were. Jessie and Ce were modern women, and modern women of the working class which made them all the more remarkable.

Ce, in particular, had a strong awareness of class. She could have gone to Roedean on a scholarship, paid by the Council, but Nanny Branch couldn't afford for her to even think about going on to a higher form of education. Ce needed to follow Jessie and go out to work to earn money at the age of fourteen. But neither Ce nor Jessie was prepared to be menial. They would be treated as equals by all those editors and journalists who had had much more education than they had had and who came from different social backgrounds.

The only problem with this, from my point of view, was that Ce was determined that I would mix easily with these people, not be embarrassed and not embarrass her. This meant that I had to speak properly, so Ce would correct the way I spoke. I had real trouble saying certain sounds – the 'th' sound, for example, and 'fire' always came out as 'far'.

Ce had trained herself to 'speak properly' and she nagged me to speak better. I resisted. We had little arguments. But we learnt to live with each other, and I think we probably moved towards each other's position and met in the middle. Thinking back, it's strange that Jessie had no real part in this. I can't remember her intervening or trying to influence the 'speaking debate' one way or the other. She spoke with a perfectly nice London accent, not as refined as Ce's, without any pretensions.

★ ★ ★

It's remarkable, really, how close we were as a family. Ce and Jessie in particular never quite accepted that we lived ten miles apart. I think in their minds that Pimlico (for Ce) and Euston, then Chalk Farm (for Jessie), were just little streets off Drury Lane where they had grown up and where Nanny Branch and Nanny Simmons still lived. Things happened that were a perfectly normal part of life then but which now – looking back – seem really strange. Why, for example, did Ce used to visit us more or less every Saturday at Levita House and do the cleaning? She would arrive and get out the dustpan and brush, mop and bucket – when Ce was around it was only a matter of minutes before the floors were wet and we were all having to walk on spread out sheets of newspaper to stop us leaving footprints everywhere. Was this just an example of the way the family was close, or did she enjoy it? Was it Nanny Branch's cleaning in the blood? Anyway I think it stopped in 1953 when Ce married Les.

Ce married Les at St Mary's Church in the Strand and I was the page boy (as the photographs show). One of the paradoxes of my early family life was the prominent part played by St Mary-le-Strand – after all, no one in the family was at all religious except Nanny Branch and hers was a religion of convenience. So here you had a big church wedding with Ce and Les, two atheists or agnostics, all for the sake of Nanny Branch who never once spoke to me of religion or belief. I was sent to a Church of England primary school – St Clements in Drury Lane – ostensibly because it fitted in with work arrangements (Jessie worked in Fleet Street, nan collected me after school). Because it was a C of E school we went regularly to church – St Mary's and Father Chambers came to teach our class every week. Despite all this I grew up blissfully ignorant of religion. My main memory of Father Chambers is him exploding with rage at me when I confessed that I didn't know who my godfather was. (I later found out that I had been christened. Mum's friend Doll Jessup was my godmother. And someone called Freddy Cox, who had been Mayor of St Pancras but had disappeared from our lives, had been my godfather.)

Anyway St Mary's continued to play a part in my life even after I left primary school in 1959. St Mary's was High Anglican, which meant it was almost Roman

Catholic in its rituals, and Nanny Branch used to go to morning communion every Sunday. By this time it was the 1960s and nan was in her seventies/eighties. She was almost blind with glaucoma and by the mid-60s she had Alzheimer's too, so she wasn't easy to look after (Ce now is uncannily like her, with her Alzheimer's). However, nan did insist on going to church even when her mind had wandered completely. The main purpose for her in going to church was to queue up afterwards for her brown envelope – all the OAPs of the parish received a charity donation (I think it was 30 shillings, so worth queuing for). Anyway Frank, Jessie and I used to arrive by car to collect nan and take her with us up to Ce's for Sunday dinner.

There was always this very practical attitude to religion in my family. Dave was the only one who really wouldn't have anything to do with it, even though he'd also gone to school at St Clements (and Ce was his godmother). The rest of us seemed to take the attitude that it was there, we might not believe in it but we might as well get what we could out of it. So, when I got into Oxford, Jessie contacted my old school and I was sent off to an interview with Mr Jones my old headmaster. I emerged from this interview with the news that the parish would give me a scholarship, worth £40 a year, to help me pay my way through Oxford. There were no religious strings attached. I took the money and ran.

When I got into Oxford it was a big, big thing for my family. I'd gone from St Clement's to William Ellis Grammar School and had never felt at ease there. It was a very middle class school, with delusions of being grander than it was. It had things like a CCF (combined cadet force) which meant that every Thursday half the school dressed up in uniform to play soldiers and drill up and down the playground. You can guess whether I took part in this or not. However, I did well academically but was always surprised at my academic success. How could I be doing better than all these bright, articulate, intelligent boys from homes wealthier than mine? Anyway, it continued and I ended up with good A-levels taken a year early, and I was told that I should stay on for Oxford entrance exams. I did that because it was easier than arguing otherwise, and then I won a scholarship to Oxford (i.e. Wadham College awarded me £60 a year – riches). The day I heard this news I went into school first thing to be told by the headmaster and I came running straight home. Jessie hadn't yet left for work, Frank hadn't yet gone to bed. It was as if they knew. Later that day a telegram arrived from Ce and Les: 'The dreaming spires will all now holler / John Simmons is an Oxford scholar.' Of course, I was proud but Jessie was prouder. She contacted the local paper which sent a reporter round to interview me – they ran a story under a headline like 'Youngest ever boy to go to Oxford' (complete lies, I was perhaps six months younger than typical). A day or two later I went up to see Nanny Branch in her flat off Drury Lane.

She'd already heard the news, via Ce or Jessie, but not quite taken it in. 'Oxford?' she asked. 'Isn't that near Chipping Norton?' Not the world's greatest traveller, one of nan's few trips outside London had been a few weeks' evacuation in the war to Chipping Norton. Both my nans used to talk about going 'over the water' when they travelled across Waterloo Bridge.

★ ★ ★

When Ce and Les got married they moved to Churchill Gardens Estate to the same flat they have now. At that time Churchill Gardens was brand new, a model estate, perhaps the first post-war council estate with properly designed children's playgrounds and up-to-date amenities like central heating supplied from Battersea Power Station over the water.

Joanna was born (Ce was 40, an unusually old first-time mother at that time) and that was great because it was like having a little sister. Although Jo was six years younger than me, my brother Dave was nine years older – and the world Jo and I had been born into was much more of the same age than the pre-war /post-war divide that separated Dave from myself. From the earliest age Jo and I were great friends – she used to visit us, but much more frequently I would go to stay with Ce and Les. It was convenient, I guess, given my mum and dad's work arrangements.

In the school holidays, on a Monday or Tuesday,
I would get on the 24 bus and travel to Pimlico.
I would stay with Ce and Les until Thursday or
Friday. Of course, Ce worked too – five days a week,
like Jessie a secretary on the newspapers. Les worked
– at night, as a printer, just like my dad. So this
meant that Jo and I got on with things, having each
other for company. I can remember Nanny Branch
being around a bit. After lunch we would go out for
a walk to Battersea Park or Chelsea Gardens. It was
always good walking on the ironwork of Chelsea
Bridge. I enjoyed those days, they were very happy
ones and I can't remember being homesick at all –
after all Ce and Les were as close as my closest family.
The only time I can remember feeling at all sad
was one New Year's Eve when I couldn't get off to
sleep and the horns of the tugbboats on the Thames
sounded especially mournful. But I've always hated
New Year.

★ ★ ★

But how to bring this to a conclusion – at least for
the time being? Let me tell you a bit about Jessie in
her last year, because in many ways that's still the
memory that stays freshest.

Having said that, there are so many details that I
can no longer remember. For example, when did
she first tell me – or did Frank tell me – that she
had cancer? You would imagine that that memory
would be indelible, but it's gone. Jessie had cancer for

something like three years, I think. She lived with
it, battled against it, went through operations to try
to defeat it, but was beaten by it in October 1968
when I was just starting my third year at Wadham. I
was 20. When I got into Oxford Jessie had seemed
well – at least not noticeably sick at that time. The
real sickness didn't come on until her last months, but
perhaps it was just the fact that I was away, enjoying
my new life and independence at Oxford, that meant
that I didn't notice enough.

In my first year at Oxford I brought friends home at
times – particularly Mike and Murray, but also Paul
and Vic. When Jessie died Mike and Murray came
to the funeral, not out of a wish to support me but
because they'd grown fond of Jessie too. She exuded
a warmth that was incredible, she related perfectly
to people of all ages, as long as they were genuine
themselves. One Sunday evening Murray was at our
place and the phone rang. Jessie answered it and told
Murray it was for him. She said, 'I think he thought I
was the servant.' Murray said, 'Bet it's Tony Hodges.'
It was. Tony Hodges was the Old Etonian Chairman
of Oxford University Labour Club – Murray was
the Secretary.

For Jessie the Labour Party really was a broad church.
It could encompass people like Tony Hodges, as long
as he learnt to behave properly. Every Christmas we
would have drinks at our flat with mum and dad's
friends. In fact this meant mainly Jessie's friends
because she knew just about everyone, and the circle

took in neighbours, people from work (journalists), from the local Labour Party and friends from way back. One of the old friends was Allen Hutt who at this time was Chief Sub-Editor of the *Daily Worker*, the Communist newspaper, and generally recognised as the country's leading expert on newspaper typography. As you can imagine from that Allen was someone who believed romantically in the workers but had absolutely no proletarian blood of his own. He was a great extrovert (his son was Sam Hutt aka Hank Wangford, the singing gynaecologist), and Allen would perform his party piece at Christmas. This involved Allen singing, unaccompanied, some revolutionary songs – the *Wild Colonial Boy* was his favourite.

This was always well-received except one Christmas when Cyril Herridge – chairman of our local ward Labour Party – objected that the language used was offensive to his wife Ellen (supposedly speaking on behalf of the other ladies too). Cyril was an ordinary working-class bloke. I think this puzzled Allen. Jessie understood but couldn't stand prissiness, just thought it was funny, got Allen to sing another song and somehow kept the party together (in both senses).

By the summer of 1968 Jessie was dying. She had had operations, including a hysterectomy, but in those days you didn't have much chance with cancer. By this time I had met Linda at Oxford. In the vacations she would come to our flat but a lot of the time now Jessie would be in bed resting. She had had to retire from work because of her illness, and she was given (she chose it herself) an antique diamond ring as a leaving /good luck present.

One day that summer, lying in bed, she showed me the ring and asked me about Linda. She asked me something like: 'Is it serious?' So I said, 'Yes' and Jessie let me know that, when she was dead, the ring would be mine to give Linda. Can you imagine a more powerful mixture of emotions?

At the end of the summer I returned to Oxford for Michaelmas Term. I was only about two weeks into term when I heard from Frank that the end was near, so I got permission to leave and return home. When I went to the hospital I was shocked to see the way Jessie had declined physically. She looked like a Belsen victim, shrunk to bones with skin just hanging on her, her lips enormously swollen in a face with hollow cheeks, her complexion as white as the sheet that covered her. I can't remember saying anything or hearing anything she said. I simply cried. After a while I left to go back to our flat, leaving Frank, Dave and Ce at her bedside. It seemed like only an hour or so later that they arrived home with the news that I had dreaded, Jessie was dead.

There's always a macabre humour that goes with death. It's part of the way we survive as humans. I always remember the afternoon Frank, Dave and I went to make the funeral arrangements – the Co-op Funeral Service, of course, it had to be the Co-op.

We went through all the questions, trying to be as controlled as possible about it all, as if we were filling in tax forms. The Co-op funeral director was a Dickensian character, exuding insincerity like Uriah Heep, but that goes with the job. He went through about 20 questions, writing our answers and requests down on the form – type of coffin, kind of service, number of cars and so on. He then said, 'One last question, do you have a Coop Dividend number?' The three of us, as one, immediately piped up '1257861'. Jessie would have been proud of us. And we had a good laugh.

The following July Linda and I married at Poplar Town Hall. Jessie's ring became our engagement ring. After the wedding we went back to Oxford to live because Linda still had a year to complete of her course at St Hilda's college. Six weeks after our wedding, we were woken in the middle of the night by a policeman who broke the news that Frank had had a heart attack at work and had died at Barts Hospital. He was never a man who displayed emotion easily, but he had said to me a few months before, 'I'm lost without Jessie'.

I'm sure there's much more I could tell you but I don't want to strain your patience. It's time to bring this letter to a conclusion, but how to do that? I'll simply say, 'I've seen the light of another day', but I aim to see a lot more. It's a wonderful life.

End of letter

4 Deep down things

Autobiographical writing is accessible to us all. You need never say, 'I don't know what to write about'. You need feel no compulsion to show it to anyone, you are simply writing it for yourself (or perhaps for one or two people very close to you). It can be a great way to throw off inhibitions about writing.

Of course, we all have such inhibitions. Much of my day-to-day work is persuading others to be less inhibited in their writing. For example, working on letter-writing with the customer services department of Marks & Spencer, I found through a long series of workshops that some people feel uncomfortable with my main letter-writing principle: *write as if you were speaking*. Perhaps not surprisingly the telephone team took to this with fewer inhibitions than the letter-writing team. But it seems we all have ingrained in us from deep in our schooldays a notion that a letter needs to be formal in tone. This formality is then expressed through the use of standard, archaic phrases used only in letters, never in speech. This is a subject I have explored again and again with many companies, including Cable & Wireless and Royal Mail (see Chapter 3).

If our letter-writing inhibitions are traceable back to schooldays, so too are our generally uncomfortable feelings towards poetry. In the section on Oxfam I touched on a poetry experiment I ran at work recently. I had a number of feelings: that many people are frightened by the thought of poetry; many are nervous but want to understand it and like it better; and very few feel able to respond with full emotion to poetry because of social and cultural inhibitions.

At the same time I felt that poetry could be a wonderful way of helping people to become accustomed to more emotive writing and to add a completely different dimension to writing at work. I hoped it might create some kind of bridge between personal and working lives. This was an important objective to me following the week-long immersion of about 30 of us in a cultural change programme called Breakthrough run by Dr Bart Sayle.

I asked for 'poetry volunteers' from the 200 members of the company and was pleased when 35 people responded from our offices in London and Amsterdam. I gathered the volunteers together one evening and gave the following talk. On the night the poems were read by our then evening receptionist Tony Howell, a man with a wonderful voice as those who saw him play Roger in the BBC's TV adaptation of *Wives and Daughters* will agree. When you come to the poems, read them inside your head, and read them in a wonderful voice.

Start of poetry reading

First, Tony's going to read you the poem that invited you to take part in this project. It's by W B Yeats.

He Wishes for the Cloths of Heaven

Had I the heavens' embroidered cloths,
Enwrought with golden and silver light,
The blue and the dim and the dark cloths
Of night and light and the half-light,
I would spread the cloths under your feet:

But I, being poor, have only my dreams;
I have spread my dreams under your feet;
Tread softly because you tread on my dreams.

The reason for choosing that poem was that it gave me the idea to try this experiment. I'd returned from our Breakthrough days, and when I got home a book of Yeats' poems had arrived. I opened it up and read this poem which I had never read before (although lots of other people have since told me it's their favourite poem).

What made it seem right? What makes any poetry resonate in our minds? It's partly the ability of a poet to reveal in a few words levels of meaning that are almost beyond words to say. 'Tread softly because you tread on my dreams.' I had come home from Breakthrough exhilarated and exhausted. Alongside excitement was a fear that the emotion we had generated – the hope, the belief, the trust – could all evaporate on returning to work.

'Tread softly because you tread on my dreams' expressed those feelings better than any words I could say or write. The words helped me to sustain my belief in what we had gained with Breakthrough because they gave me another endorsement of emotion itself. They recognised the fragility of all our dreams, whether those dreams relate to personal or business life.

Poetry is about expressing emotion. Wordsworth talked about poetry taking its origin 'from emotion recollected in tranquillity'. And that definition works for Wordsworth's poetry but not for every kind of poetry. Wendy Cope took a different view.

An Argument with Wordsworth

'Poetry . . . takes its origin from emotion recollected in tranquillity'
(Preface to the Lyrical Ballads)

> People are always quoting that and all of them
> seem to agree
> And it's probably most unwise to admit that
> it's different for me.
> I have emotion – no one who knows me could
> fail to detect it –
> But there's a serious shortage of
> tranquillity in which to recollect it.
> So this is my contribution to the theoretical
> debate:
> Sometimes poetry is emotion recollected in
> a highly emotional state.

We all have emotion. We're often short of tranquillity in which to recollect it – particularly when so much of our time is spent at work, where we're so much under pressure of time.

So there were two thoughts. The first was about allowing more emotion into our working life through poetry. The second was about using poetry to create a sense of tranquillity through the exploration of emotion.

The first thought seemed important because we all bring only part of ourselves to work. What we show at work is the outer person. But what is really interesting is the inner person. Can we find ways to bring more of the inner person to work? If so, will we be more fulfilled in our total life? If so, will we actually do better work because much of our work needs to have an emotional content?

The second thought is about finding, or creating, the time and space to think. I've been increasingly aware that I don't have enough time to think and, if I'm not thinking, I'm not doing my job very well. We all need to think but perhaps we get out of the habit of thinking as we become used to certain ways of doing things. Formulas – which sometimes we call 'experience' – mean that we do things in certain ways because we know those ways worked before. I personally need to challenge myself to think differently and not to rely on old formulas. And perhaps we all need to, and perhaps poetry is one way we can introduce new thinking into our minds. This poem is by Leonard Cohen.

The Only Poem

This is the only poem
I can read

I am the only one
can write it
I didn't kill myself
when things went wrong
I didn't turn
to drugs or teaching
I tried to sleep
but when I couldn't sleep
I learned to write
I learned to write
what might be read
on nights like this
by one like me

The important thing to realise about poetry is that you don't read it for a defined meaning. Each of us will approach any poem with our own individual emotions and thoughts — and in doing so we will make something of that poem that becomes completely individual to us.

Poetry is unlike other forms of writing. It is not about clarity although it can help you to clarify your thoughts. And, strangely, a poem can be both intensely personal, written for the poet as well as by the poet, and completely universal. There is something in the intensity of emotion put into the poem by the poet that enables each of us to relate to it in an individual way.

This is what I think Raymond Carver is saying in this poem.

107

Poems

They've come every day this month.
Once I said I wrote them because
I didn't have time for anything
else. Meaning, of course, better
things – things other than mere
poems and verses. Now I'm writing
them because I want to.
More than anything because
this is February
when normally not much of anything
happens. But this month
the larches have blossomed,
and the sun has come out
every day. It's true my lungs
have heated up like ovens.
And so what if some people
are waiting for the other shoe
to drop, where I'm concerned.
Well, here it is then. Go ahead.
Put it on. I hope it fits
like a shoe.
Close enough, yes, but supple
so the foot has room to breathe
a little. Stand up. Walk
around. Feel it? It will go
where you're going, and be there
with you at the end of your trip.
But for now, stay barefoot. Go
outside for a while, and play.

I hope that by giving you these examples I can start to help you explore some of the emotions and thoughts that I'd like this experiment to initiate. The important things that poetry is about are to do with emotion and thought, whereas for most people – perhaps going back to schooldays – poetry is about external features like rhyme and thumpety rhythm. Great poets often use these external features to give extra meaning and emotion to their writing, but these features do not themselves define poetry.

If there are going to be 35 of us taking part in this experiment, we're going to work with different approaches to poetry. Some of the poems will rhyme, some won't. Each poem will have a different kind of metre – i.e. rhythm will be varied. One overriding piece of advice is simply to listen to the poetry – listen as it is read out loud, listen inside your head as you read it to yourself.

I've chosen poems for each of you. I've made some attempt to match them to my views of your different personalities – but please don't read too much meaning into that. I've tried above all to choose poems that can have universal meaning, and I've been driven by two principles – diversity and discovery. These principles are my answer to those who complained that they would rather choose their own poem. If everyone had chosen their own favourite poem, I've no doubt that we would have found fewer opportunities to discover new things about poetry and about ourselves. And almost certainly the overall diversity would have been reduced too.

Discovery and diversity are also words that became important to us during Breakthrough.

In a little while I'll give each of you a poem that I've selected for you. You might or might not know the poem. Whether you know it or not, I'd like you to get to know that poem extremely well over the coming weeks. The meaning of poetry doesn't always come easily. It's not like translation. The meaning might be different to you on different days.

Get to know your poem well. Read it out loud, read it inside your head. Read the poem every day. And as the days go by, you'll get a little bit more meaning all the time.

If you'd like my help to explore the poem, I'll be happy to do so. But don't expect me to tell you what the poem's meaning is – the only meaning is the poem's meaning to you.

And that's what I'd like to hear, and what I'd like to read. In a month's time, I'd like you to have written down your thoughts on the poem. What does it mean to you? What insights has it given you into your life? Has it told you anything new about the person that you are, about the world, about your role in the world, about the things that matter to you in life, at home, at work? Have individual words or phrases developed special meaning for you? Has the poem changed the way you think? Has it influenced your own writing at all?

Perhaps, too, in response to the last question, think about the way you write your own response. We're not after a business proposal here. Take the chance to enjoy using language which expresses emotion, allow language to develop your thinking. The more you do that, the more you'll enjoy it.

To finish what I want to say, Tony's going to give you a poem by Gwendolyn MacEwen called *Let me make this perfectly clear.*

> Let me make this perfectly clear.
> I have never written anything because it is
>   a Poem.
> This is a mistake you always make about me,
> A dangerous mistake. I promise you
> I am not writing this because it is a Poem.
>
> You suspect this is a posture or an act.
> I am sorry to tell you it is not an act.
>
> You actually think I care if this
> Poem gets off the ground or not. Well
> I don't care if this poem gets off the ground
>   or not
> And neither should you.
> All I have ever cared about
> And all you should ever care about

Is what happens when you lift your eyes
from this page.

Do not think for one minute it is the Poem
    that matters.
It is not the Poem that matters.
You can shove the Poem.
What matters is what is out there in the
    large dark
And in the long light,
Breathing.

End of poetry reading

What was the effect of the poetry experiment? The 35 people took their poems away and lived with them for a while. A few decided that that was enough and wrote nothing in response. Some people wrote little, saying simple things like, 'Thank you. I now think of this as my poem.' One person wrote about using the poem daily as a transition between leaving work and arriving home as a mother ready to look after a young child. Others described a changing relationship between the reader and the poem as meaning changed over time. Some took very personal meanings out of the poems, relating them to their lives. One person credited his poem with making him give up smoking. And others bared their souls with tremendous courage and exposed black demons in their lives – which the poems helped them to fight against.

I have tried not to claim too much for this experiment, but it was a moving experience. Yet it was an experience that I felt should not be repeated – at least, not with this same group of people. It seemed to me that this idea should not be institutionalised into a formal 'poetry club' meeting regularly and swapping views on poems. I had intended it to be more deeply personal than that and I had succeeded. Now I did not want to risk destroying the momentary beauty of the idea, its brief snowdrop existence. But I remain convinced that this idea can be replicated in other organisations and bring about a deep change in attitudes to the benefit of individuals and the organisations.

The poetic moment did live on in people's minds. Rita Clifton, our chief executive, had been one of the 35 volunteers and she had responded enthusiastically to her poem – Maya Angelou's *Still I Rise*. This led to a final flowering of the poetic idea when Rita asked me if I could make our company mission and vision statement into a poem for the Interbrand Group conference. I resisted this idea for a while, not wanting to become the company laureate commissioned to write odes for special occasions. In the end I decided I could do it if I made the poem personal by taking the spirit of the mission / vision statement and using none of the original words. So, without a mention of brands, this was the poem.

Each day
we start a new life.

We are seekers of possibilities
finders of likely ideas
in unlikely places.

We know we can change the world
because
we can change
the way we see the world.

Think of the things
we can do.
We can
because we believe
we can.
So do.

I was pleased when, in 2004, the poem found new life and meaning. As part of an initiative called 'The Big Sing', the poem became a song. The aim of the Big Sing was to draw attention to the importance of music in education. Set to music by the composer Alec Roth, the song was sung by thousands of children in schools around the UK.

3 THEM

IS THERE ANYONE OUT THERE?

'All this will not be
finished in the first
100 days. Nor will it
be finished in the first
1000 days, nor in the life
of this Administration,
nor even perhaps in
our lifetime on this
planet. But let
us begin.'

John F Kennedy

1 Core audiences

In this chapter I will look at writing through the perspective of the audience. One thing that people seem to be clear about, particularly people who are not natural writers, is that you have to remember that you are writing for a specific audience. It's a fundamental part of the briefing process for any form of marketing communications – who is the audience?

Defining the audience – or at least having an idea in your head of a person that you are writing for – is helpful for a writer. We all need reminding that words are dead until they are read.

Awareness of the audience also shapes the way we write and the words we use. Sometimes lack of awareness of the real audience influences our words. Rather than talking to customers in the language of customers, a company might adopt the language of its suppliers and simply assume that customers relate to this language as easily as the company's own buyers do. This is what I believe happened with the UK's leading retailer Marks & Spencer in the 1990s. It became increasingly inward-focused and assumed that technical details of fabrics, for example, were more important to customers than style and glamour. So 'machine washable' and 'non-iron' became more acceptable descriptions at the point of sale than 'looks good'.

In that case, the linguistic influence at the core of the company was the suppliers'. As Marks & Spencer attempts to recover its position in the market, it will try to restore the customer as the greatest influence on its everyday language. This might be expressed as moving from diagram *A* to *B*.

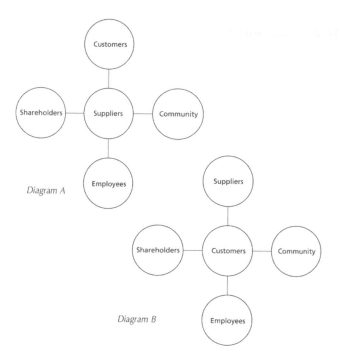

Diagram A

Diagram B

In these diagrams the other 'satellite' audience groups are important but they are not the dominant influence on the company's tone of voice. Other companies might have variations on these diagrams, with different audience groups at the core. Most companies today would probably claim that the customer is always at the core, but the reality is often different. Many companies, for example, have their shareholders at the core and the need to address this audience has a magnetic pull on the company's language. You can supply your own examples, whichever part of the world you think about, and the examples are not necessarily confined to financial service companies.

Sometimes companies deliberately put 'unusual' audiences at their core; this then influences the tone of voice and is a major differentiator of the brand. For example, the advertising agency St Luke's might have 'our own people' at its core – because that was the way it was set up, the way it continues to run and the reason for its success in separating itself from its competitors.

A company's understanding of its core audiences, and its relationship with that group, will therefore have a pervasive influence on its language and on its brand. With brands we are concerned primarily with differentiation; we want to find ways to show that the experience you will have with us is significantly different from the experience you will have with any of our competitors.

I work for a brand consultancy. Ironically companies in this business are not immune from making the same kind of mistake I have talked about above. We have often used language that makes more sense to us than to our clients. Let me be honest and discuss some of that language while admitting that the discussion will not be resolved in this book – yet it has to be exposed to set this chapter in context.

As stated above, I work for a brand consultancy. Some years ago, when part of the same company, we described ourselves as a corporate identity consultancy. The world changes, or at least the words we use to describe the world change. As a corporate identity consultancy we used to devote a lot of energy to saying things like: 'A logo is not an identity. Identity is about more than just the visual means that you use to represent your company.' Then we would work on that company's identity, concentrating inevitably on the visual elements such as the logo, symbol, colours, typefaces, use of photography or illustration. Such is the power of visual imagery that this approach often brought about far-reaching changes for the companies adopting new visual identities.

Increasingly, though, it became clear that the argument to portray corporate identity as 'more than just a logo' was making snail-like progress both within the design industry (because many designers just love and understand the visual) and among the industry's clients and potential clients (many of whom simply did not have the experience or the imagination to know that this 'identity process' could reach into every corner of the company). For a large number of client companies, identity was simply a control mechanism – 'let's get everything consistent' – rather than the catalyst to unlock a company's creative energy. Enormous, weighty tomes called Corporate Identity Manuals were produced to codify everything that could be stamped with a logo – and, presumably, to come down hard on the heads of those who broke the rules.

Companies such as ours were trying to pioneer a different approach to corporate identity, using a word like 'diversity' rather more admiringly than 'uniformity'. As one of the people in the company who was not a designer by training, and as someone who cared about the language that we used, I was responsible for writing many of the words that described this approach to identity. As a company involved in identity programmes that seemed to have an increasingly global reach – working for British Airways, for example, newly merged companies like Pharmacia & Upjohn and PricewaterhouseCoopers – we knew that visual imagery had enormous power. But we were often frustrated because our specialism – described as corporate identity – was perceived as much narrower than our ambitions for it. For myself, as a writer, I grew frustrated that a company's use of language was rarely seen as an identity issue.

In 1997 the company I was part of, Newell and Sorrell, merged with Interbrand. It was a good merger because the two companies' skills fitted together, but the locus for Interbrand's approach can be gleaned from its name. 'Brand' is the key word in Interbrand's vocabulary and, after a year of skirmishing about terminology, brand is now used by us all to describe what our business is about. We still use the word 'identity' but we generally precede it with the word 'visual' to denote logos, symbols, colours and other graphic elements. Yet for me, as a writer, identity has continuing resonance because it suggests that what we are on the inside is inextricably linked to the way we appear on the outside.

What has happened is that the word 'brand' has changed in meaning over a couple of decades. A brand once meant the names and imagery which described consumer products like M&Ms, Daz and Bovril. Now even the companies which own these consumer product brands believe that the most important brand is the company itself. So, if the company is the brand, it's obvious that the company is made up of people as well as products – and the behaviour of those people represents the brand to all the brand's stakeholders.

121

Clearly, if we are going to address brand issues in the most fundamental sense, we have to address behaviour and the values which lie behind a company's behaviour and which represent the brand. You cannot do these things without seriously considering the brand's 'tone of voice', the way it demonstrates its values through the words that are written and spoken by the people who represent the brand.

I have used the word 'stakeholder', a term that came to the fore in the 1990s. I suspect it might not remain with us very much longer because it is in some ways a dishonest, presumptuous word. Am I a stakeholder in a company simply because I receive direct mail from it? Am I a stakeholder if I am a disaffected employee? Or am I called a stakeholder simply because the company wants to pretend that I am every bit as important as a shareholder – but don't let the shareholders know!

I have a belief that it would be better to go back to a word that has had currency for far longer and that implies the need for a communicative relationship. I believe we should in fact talk about 'audiences' because there is no doubt that any brand wants its message to be heard. The audiences are out there, waiting to listen – whether they are customers, suppliers, local communities or a company's own people. They are the 'them' of the book's title and this chapter's title.

A brand wants its messages to be heard – and understood. How can words be seen as unimportant in that scenario? Yet it is only in relatively recent times that the question of a brand's tone of voice has been a matter for serious consideration. It matters because words send signals, and they can be sending the right signals or the wrong ones. Whether they are right or wrong depends on the way they are received by the audiences who hear or read them. But we have to admit that there is this possibility of taking words the right way or the wrong way.

In the rest of this chapter, I describe how tone of voice works in practice through case studies and examples of work with different brands. In each case the company has recognised the importance of words in communicating with key audiences, but I would regard each example as 'work in progress'.

2 Words are made of letters: Royal Mail

I have known Royal Mail as one of my clients for nearly 20 years, but of course our real relationship has existed for my whole life. I'm sure that the day after I was born a friendly postman must have delivered cards and letters to my mum and dad. Despite occasional evidence to the contrary, we still think of the postman or postwoman as friendly. That is a wonderful asset and heritage for any brand to own.

The warmth of these feelings towards the brand was strengthened for me by the work that I did for Royal Mail over many years, creating programmes for teachers and young people. Whether through educational materials that went into schools, or through letter-writing competitions that were entered by hundreds of thousands of young people, I was helping Royal Mail to demonstrate its support of the written word. There was a happy coincidence between educational needs and corporate objectives. Royal Mail, as the organisation which delivers written words through your letterbox, has an obvious interest in promoting literacy. Altruism and business sense both point in the same direction – and that's a rare combination.

You might reasonably wonder whether the young letter-writers in schools today will still be sending letters in 20 years' time. Electronic communication – and the e-mail is only a recent competitor – threatened the death of the letter through the whole of the last century. Yet, remarkably, the volume of mail continues to rise. This might not be because we all continue to write letters to each other, but we are certainly receiving and reading more written communications than we did before. It seems that all communication is benignly complimentary. Telephones encourage the use of the mail and vice versa.

Having said that, there is no doubt that Royal Mail is under greater competitive pressure than at any other time in its history (and this is a company that goes back centuries). Changing social, educational and workplace behaviour is one threat but increasing direct competition from other mail carriers has loomed in recent years. You then need to add the uncertain relationship with government, forever considering whether to change the nature and ownership of the company, from public to private and points in between. These and many other factors have meant that Royal Mail needed to ask questions about its brand. What does it really stand for? Does it need clarifying? Is it equipped for the changing competitive situation?

We were asked to carry out a brand audit in 1998 and I led the team. It was clear that there was much about the visible expressions of the Royal Mail brand that could not be changed. Royal Mail's symbol, the cruciform incorporating the crown, was almost literally imbedded in the physical infrastructure of the UK. Many companies talk fancifully about 'owning' a colour, but Royal Mail through its ubiquitous vans and pillar boxes had more claim than anyone else to owning the colour red. So the visual icons of the brand were strong, even if there were issues to do with the way the visual identity was implemented and managed.

Our main client was a forceful, determined woman called Deborah Gildea, Royal Mail's head of brand management. Deborah understood that the brand is in the detail but refused to be daunted by the mass of details that every day chipped away at the brand. These details might be battered vehicles, sloppy uniforms, wrongly delivered letters and often appalling industrial relations, particularly affecting the front-line employees in the sorting and delivery offices.

Of course, it all came down to behaviour. How did Royal Mail expect its people to treat customers? How did Royal Mail managers behave towards employees? These were enormous issues which the brand audit could not solve but could only highlight. The solutions needed to focus on changing behaviour, making it possible for people to be proud to work for Royal Mail, but any changes would take years to work through. The brand programme was one of several change programmes all pushing in the same direction towards a fitter company.

In looking at Royal Mail communications, as part of the brand audit, we concluded that Royal Mail could radically improve the quality of its printed material without changing any of the permanent visual elements of the brand. One way to bring about such improvement was through concentrating on tone of voice, making sure that the written and spoken voice of Royal Mail reflected the core, differentiating values that we had identified in the brand audit. Put simply, write better – write in a way that projects the brand values you wish to project.

Of course, there were problems with this approach. The people responsible for writing the words in Royal Mail printed materials were not necessarily good writers. As in many other organisations, words were neglected. There was a concentration on getting facts and information across, whereas you need emotion to communicate effectively. Even when outside agencies were used to write materials, the writers employed were often designers who knew first and foremost that they had to fill the type columns with words that would help their designs to look good.

Deborah Gildea asked me to address an audience of Royal Mail communication executives and representatives from the vastly reduced number of agencies who now made up Royal Mail's design roster. This is what I said to them about Royal Mail's tone of voice.

Start of letter

'Dear Deborah,

Many thanks for asking me to speak today. I thought I'd write you a letter instead. As you know, we recommended that Royal Mail's tone of voice should be like that of an informal letter... so it just seemed the right thing to do.

Although the letter is written to you, I've copied it to all our colleagues here. And, although I address it to you, don't take it too personally – I'm afraid you have to stand in for the whole of Royal Mail.

I'm particularly grateful to you for asking me because, as you know, I'm passionate about words.

And I believe Royal Mail should be passionate about words too. After all they are your business.

I've always thought and said that if any company in the country needs to care for the written word, that company is Royal Mail. The written word is your business, and your future business depends on people agreeing with a proposition like 'a letter says it best'.

What I'd like you to do – and like us all to do – is practise what we preach. How often do we write letters to each other? I've worked with Royal Mail for years but received fewer letters from Royal Mail than from many other businesses I deal with. Why is this? Is it a lack of confidence in your own medium? We all need to believe in this medium, and we all need to believe in the power of words as a way to express your brand.

But don't just take my word for it. Words matter, words are at the heart of business.

'Businesses are made of ideas – ideas expressed as words.'

James Champy

Now we all know that words don't always convey ideas well. When words are used badly, they can confuse, mislead and simply baffle us. I'm going to look at some examples from Royal Mail, some examples gathered over the last few months.

I was interested to see from *South East News* that Royal Mail now has a Trauma Care Programme – shortened to TCP, of course. Apparently 'the most obvious event likely to cause trauma is a physical attack or violent verbal abuse'.

So we all know and recognise that words can traumatise us and that words can damage your health. I also believe that words can be used to improve your health. We'll look at both situations. When we began working on the Brand Audit at the beginning of the year, our relationship didn't get off to the raciest start, although I'm sure it was legally proper. I mean, of course, that we got a contract.

If we followed the definition of terms in the contract: 'Contract means an agreement between the Post Office and the Contractor for the supply of design services which is stated to be subject to the General Conditions, and which may incorporate a Brief, or Specification or Proposal and other special conditions.'

OK, I know it's the law and all that, but we're asked to sign contracts which use this kind of language – 15 pages worth of it – and few of us can understand a word of them.

Does it matter? After all, it's only lawyers talking to lawyers. But I think it matters because if the brand character is about 'helping relationships' we should start as we mean to go on – by working to understand each other. And the brand can't stop operating when it reaches certain departments.

Anyway, we soon put the terms of the contract behind us. For most of us, the brief is the kick-off for any job. How good are your briefs? The honest answer is 'variable', and I'll be interested to hear what others think. My personal view is that a written brief should be just that – brief. You shouldn't try to cover every angle in a written brief.

We had one brief that said: 'Everything needs to be communicated.' Well, the answer to the mystery of the Universe is '42'. Does that cover everything?

The words were simple enough there, it was the thought that was confused. Sometimes briefs use words in a baffling way. For example: 'The behaviour aspects of operating in a matrix culture need to be stated and "felt".'

What does that mean? There's a terrible danger in putting words together in combinations that give a veneer of management consultancy respectability – but actually they mean very little. We called our Brand Audit report 'The simpler the better' because that is a piece of advice that applies generally to Royal Mail. Take this brief: 'It is anticipated that the model will be developed for use solely by Royal Mail and will not be a modification of an existing model where the rights are assigned to someone else.'

OK, you'd like the model to be yours. The simpler the better.

Part of the complication comes from the assumed need to sound 'important'. I wish people in Royal Mail didn't feel the need to sound posh.

A sure sign of this posturing is the use of passive rather than active verbs, and the avoidance of personal pronouns. Instead of 'It is anticipated' it's much better to say 'We anticipate'.

There are other examples of course. 'Utilisation' and 'utilise' are favourite Royal Mail words. Why not use 'use'? Do you have to 'undertake' something, when you could 'do' it instead? 'It is envisaged' is a pompous way to say 'We think'.

Those are a few suggestions, but this isn't meant to be a guideline, it's simply a letter with some observations.

I'm much happier when Royal Mail has a lighter touch and shows that it has a sense of humour. Like the shot in the 'Your new look' brochure showing a postman in new uniform with some sheep in a field behind him. And the note beside them reads: 'I saw this and thought of ewe.' It's a good quality to be able to laugh at yourself.

131

When you write for yourselves, for example in publications like *The Business*, sometimes you can get weighed down by your own bureaucracy and that stifles understanding as well as humour. Listen to this: 'Following completion of the initial statements, involvement is being broadened to get input from other key stakeholders in Royal Mail.' That's good, you're asking people. It goes on: 'The refined strategic statements will form the basis of any adjustments needed to RMEC's way of working, Royal Mail's management approach, and realignments of the planning process and organisational development in support of a defined business direction.' Sorry, you lost me there. I said 'listen' deliberately. One piece of advice I absolutely believe in is simply this – when you've written something, read it through again (inside your head, if you like) and listen. Listen, for example, to the way you run out of breath half way through that last sentence. And when I say 'you' I mean any one of us.

If this sounds critical of Royal Mail, it is – but you're not alone and I don't think any of your competitors are significantly better. Here's a chance to gain competitive advantage by focusing on this area where we could make big improvements.

Some of your competitors are DHL, UPS and TNT – which I find ironic given Royal Mail's fondness for using initials. You have to be careful that your internal jargon, abbreviations and acronyms don't find their way out into the wider world. RMN,

RMS and RMI are weaker competitors to DHL, UPS and TNT than Royal Mail.

I see that one idea submitted to 'Melting Pot' (your suggestion scheme) was: 'Produce a list of all the Royal Mail abbreviations and what they stand for.' A good idea and a bad idea. Imagine the size of the book and the amount of paper. It will fall foul of your environmental policy on paper – some effort made here with words: 'Refuse Reduce Reuse Recycle'.

For example, did you know that MIPP is Managing the Integrated Product Pipeline, Key Interface Measures are KIMs, and BER is the Business Excellence Review. All of these come under UX, which stands for Unit Excellence. I think it would be excellent business practice to cut all these abbreviations out. KO rather than OK.

The problem is that they depersonalise and dehumanise. I see that in Royal Mail you have 'People Change Managers'. I'm not sure if that's a job title or a revolutionary slogan, but it's apparently part of the 'People Project'.

It's great to have a People Project but let's try to talk to people as if they really are people. You've got heroes and heroines out there doing great jobs every day, and you recognise many of these people with awards. 'William Cluckie, postman of Newton, for dressing up as Postman Pat to raise money for cancer relief.' He definitely deserved a medal for that.

But unfortunately we didn't genuinely care enough about A. Byers, M. Johnstone, J. Marrs and many others to find out what their first names were.

And people are the clue to all this. If we genuinely care, and that's the key value of the brand, we have to care for people. Those inside the company, those outside the company. We have to care for their needs. They will certainly need to understand. They also need to feel cared for.

Let me round this up with a brief look at one booklet that we've worked on that shows the difference words can make. Particularly when the words are combined with some good imagery.

This booklet used to be called 'Our service standards' and probably at that time the use of 'our' was something of a breakthrough. We renamed the booklet 'We want to help you' and that clearly shows the direction in which we were heading.

Throughout the booklet we moved away from the previous kind of monumental headings in boxes – saying 'OUR SERVICE STANDARDS', 'OUR COMPENSATION POLICY', 'OUR CONDITIONS OF SERVICES' etc – to conversational sentences that lead you into the main copy – 'You expect reliable service . . . and, of course, you should receive just that'.

Writing the words for this booklet was not easy,
simply because so many people were involved.
We had to clear the words both with the Legal
Department and POUNC, the consumer watchdog.
One comment from POUNC was: 'This section is
a bit "chatty" and, as a result, somewhat misleading
in terms of what RM is required to do.' (Notice the
RM seeping out.)

That comment seemed to be the crux of the
problem. Is this a legal document (in which case no
one will understand it) or is it a genuine attempt
to give customer service (in which case we have to
make sure that customers can understand it)?

We veered towards the latter, rather than coming
down on the side of the law. We didn't think it
should be about 'requirements'. We decided it should
be about what Royal Mail is trying to do to
help customers.

And there's a truth in that. We found out by
spending a day in the London Customer Service
Centre, listening and talking to people. One of the
things we decided to do was use their own words, as
quotations, and put their real names to the quotations
(with their agreement, of course).

So we had Lisa Dinnick saying: 'I always make sure
that the caller gets my full name. There are over 200
of us here, and that means there are a lot of Lisas...'
Rather than just leave it as a statement in the text we

personalised this quotation by attributing it to Julie
Livingston: 'It's always good to get comments
from customers.'

There are all these conversations going on out there.
They're real people, talking in the way real people
talk – the way that Royal Mail needs to talk in its
written style. We need to find ways to bring that out
in all the projects that we work on. Don't ignore the
words – let's all take it as our responsibility to make
them work as hard as they can.

Let's help our own people too, as much as we can.
For example, those people in the Customer Service
Centres talk on the phone to customers and they
handle those calls brilliantly. Do we give them the
backing they need from the forms that they use, for
example? Your own staff have to fill in a section
that says: 'Please specify a reason/problems and what
action has been taken to rectify problems/failures.'
That language immediately makes people respond in
the same style, in the language of bureaucracy.

We should be simpler. We should ask: 'What went
wrong and what have you done to put things right?'

I'll stop there, because that seems a good question to
end with and to make sure that we do challenge, that
we do try to make things better.

With best wishes
John Simmons'

End of letter

I cannot claim that my work on tone of voice has revolutionised Royal Mail. This is one of the biggest companies in the UK, employing a couple of hundred thousand people. A revolution would need to mobilise, in what already seems the quaint language of a previous century, 'propaganda to precipitate a mass movement'. *This* cultural revolution was low-key, trying to work almost by stealth, spreading out in ripples from the centre. And it continues.

3 Pulling out words: Anglia Railways

We had worked with InterCity (British Rail's long-distance passenger service) for many years before the British railways were privatised in the 1990s. One of our clients at InterCity had been Andy Cooper and, in the new set-up of privatised rail companies, Andy became managing director of Anglia Railways whose trains ran on the main line between London- Liverpool Street and Norwich, and all around East Anglia on branch lines.

Andy was a rarity among managing directors. He actually believed that words matter. Like all MDs of the newly privatised companies he had to run a cost-conscious operation, but he was prepared to invest in words. Anglia's customer service director, Tim Clarke, also believed that the company could give a better experience to customers if it used words more effectively.

So I packed my bags and went off by train around East Anglia, meeting people in the stations, listening to announcements on trains, reading information displays and leaflets and talking to a cross-section of Anglia Railways' staff. John Prideaux, who had been managing director of InterCity, used to start speeches by saying, 'I like trains'. I share that liking. But too often communication at railway stations is accurately and funnily summed up by the scene at the start of Jacques Tati's *M Hulot's Holiday*. As passengers wait on the platform, an unintelligible announcement is made, someone seems to understand and leads a rush to the platform on the other side of the tracks; the train then pulls up at the now-empty platform where everyone had previously been waiting; the train pulls out empty. Here was a challenge. How can this be improved? Given a liking for trains, it was a challenge I wanted to meet. I carried out my research then presented the following report to Anglia Railways.

Start of report

Along the way

As I have gone around speaking to Anglia people, I have been collecting examples of written and spoken words, ranging from customer letters to station displays, scripts for train announcements to printed marketing material, training documents to staff newspapers.

From personal observation rather than from any exhaustive competitive analysis, Anglia Railways does relatively well in these areas. The fact that you have asked for this report says a lot about your recognition of the importance of tone of voice. But more importantly the system that you have already set up argues for your commitment. With 22,000 customers contacting you in a year, and 22,000 written replies, the importance of written communication is clear.

But of course you can improve.

It is fundamentally to do with your culture. As you know, cultural changes are needed and there is no ready acceptance of the need for change. During the few short weeks of this research, resistance to change became evident from the absence of any announcements on the journey. If train drivers, for example, resist the idea of speaking to customers through PA announcements, it is clear that there is some way to go before teamworking and customer service are seen as drivers of the business.

'People have a resistance to new ideas that don't use the vernacular. They say, "It's not for us".'

In trying to bring about any improvements in tone of voice we therefore need to be practical. We need to take a number of steps, not necessarily consecutive. I summarise these as:

- *Deal with practical issues that harm your tone of voice (your PA systems need improvement)*

- *Improve the formal written word by making it sound more informal – in your letters (small improvements possible) and in your scripts (big improvements possible)*

- *Train people to feel more comfortable with words (both written and spoken)*

- *Make it clear that this is an issue that relates absolutely to key service and operational issues (for example, customer relations and teamworking)*

- *Make a commitment to being the leader in your industry in the use of words — make it a key element of your identity*

- *Clarify the idea behind your tone of voice (first say that it matters, then say why it matters uniquely to Anglia Railways)*

- *Find ways to express that idea — and constantly find new ways to keep expressing it.*

Pulling in for a while

I've raced through a whole set of actions, a bit like the old film of the London to Brighton train journey in five minutes. Let's slow down and go back to some broad thoughts about train travel and about Anglia.

First, there's the fact that you are in an unusual position – compared to any of the other privatised rail companies – in having a clearly defined region. This gives you an advantage that can be developed further in the future.

Secondly, rail travel has its own special characteristics and the balance is turning much more towards the train as a means of travel that has real advantages. If government increasingly sees these advantages in a political and economic context – in opposition to road building, as an environmental preference – other key audiences see rail's advantages in the context of quality of life. This applies to business customers – 'It's less stressful and more productive to take the train'– and to leisure/obligatory customers – 'I'd rather relax and enjoy the journey'. Rail travel can be much better than simply a means to get from A to B.

The opportunity for Anglia is in truly recognising this and demonstrating its understanding. Part of the answer comes from the way you demonstrate that understanding – largely through a clear, purposeful use of appropriate words in different situations.

The answer also comes from associating yourself clearly with the idea of enjoying language and being committed to fostering its developing use as a differentiator for your company.

Taking a journey

The assumption behind the last section was that rail travel can be, indeed should be, the most relaxing way to travel. It has fewer anxieties and discomforts than its main competitors, the car and the plane.

But rail travel does have anxieties of its own and it's important to recognise these, so that we can address them.

With air travel the anxiety is about getting there safely. This is the base anxiety that communication on a plane is designed to quell – i.e. the safety procedures on video and in person, the captain's reassuring presence on the intercom. Without this anxiety at least being recognised, there would be no opportunity to turn to more positive aspects of customer service – 'Would you like a drink / headphones/ peanuts etc?'

With rail travel the anxiety is of a different kind, less intense, but universal. The concern is mainly about getting to the right place at about the right time. It's almost impossible to get on a plane to the wrong destination. It's only too easy to get on the wrong train or to get off at the wrong stop.

'Oh Mr Porter, what shall I do? I wanted to go to Birmingham and they've taken me on to Crewe...'

How should we address this anxiety? There are simple things that can be considered, all to do with the use of words. For example:

- *Before the doors close, before the train sets off, there should always be an announcement. 'This is the 10:45 to Lowestoft, stopping at Westerfield etc.' This would prevent passengers taking the 10:41 to Felixstowe by mistake (I realised and got off at Westerfield).*

- *After the train has stopped at a station and pulled out, say 'This train will stop at . . . ' (local service) or 'Our next stop will be Stowmarket in about 15 minutes' (InterCity).*

- *On InterCity services, having a prestopping announcement before every stop. For example: 'We will be arriving at Ipswich in five minutes. Five minutes to Ipswich'. This should be said very straightforwardly – there's no flamboyance needed. Ideally it will be spoken by the driver, which will reinforce the impression that you are totally in control of what matters most to your customers – destination and timing. It then allows them to feel in control as a result because you've given them the information they need.*

I know there will be practical issues against some of these ideas – to do with job definitions, time available and, not least, the risk of irritating regular customers while you try to please irregular ones. My view is that the regular customer will not be irritated if announcements are kept short and factual – they will screen out information that is unnecessary to them.

'Would you like any refreshments?'

Customers are far more likely to be irritated by announcements that are seen to be driven by your needs (e.g. the need to earn money by selling 'refreshments') than by their needs (get me there on time). Many people on a train will not want to buy from the buffet or the trolley or the restaurant car; everyone wants to get to their destination.

So it's important to get the tone of voice right for catering announcements. As well as having the aim of not irritating customers, these announcements have the aim of selling. It's much better to do it well.

The formal script for PA announcements is right in recognising the priority – conductor first, catering second. The script is not necessarily intended as a word-by-word prompt to be read out, although there is a clear expectation that the script will be followed unless there's a very good reason not to.

This would be fine if the script were perfect, but it isn't. The script seems to me to betray its British Rail origins, and at times speaks in the language of petty bureaucracy. If it were written in a way that was close to real speech, it would be easier to read by staff and less grating for customers. The script could be rewritten in a more accessible tone of voice. Let me give a few examples:

Current script	*Suggested examples*
Purchase	**Buy**
Beverage	**Drink**
Providing us with your comments	**Making comments**
I am pleased to inform you that we will offer a full buffet service on board	**Today we've got a full buffet service**
We have available	**We have**
… are also available	**We also have**

I look forward to being of service to you again	**I hope to see you again**
Your assistance in keeping aisles clear of luggage would be appreciated	**Please help us by keeping aisles clear of luggage**

The current tone veers towards Uriah Heep mixed with 1960s Odeon advertising. 'For a full meal or just a snack, our theatre restaurant is at your service.'

Getting back on track

Let's return to the steps suggested earlier:

• **Deal with the practical issues that harm your tone of voice**
Your on-train PA systems are poor, particularly on local trains. Often it is impossible to hear announcements when they are made.

• **Improve the formal written word by making it sound more informal**
Your letters are generally good, but improvements could be made. Of course many letters have to be standard (it couldn't be otherwise with 22,000 a year) but it would be worth sharpening and polishing each of the standard letters to get rid of occasional stiffness. This could be achieved as a workshop with existing customer relations staff. The scripted announcements on trains have greater scope for improvement. These should be changed as soon as possible.

- **Train people to feel more comfortable with words**

  The existing training materials and schemes are good. The focus on customer service provides a good grounding in getting people to think in the language of the customer – i.e. what does the customer want to know rather than what do I want to tell the customer? Additional focus on tone of voice can be built into existing materials. Give more attention to training people to deliver words effectively – there's too much gabbling at the moment.

- **Make it clear that this is an issue that relates absolutely to key service and operational issues**

  If 'our people represent the difference' then they must express that difference in the way they speak and write. For some the culture shock will be that they are expected to speak to customers. Stories were reported to me of, for example, drivers keeping themselves to themselves and feeling no responsibility to talk to customers. I believe drivers are the best people on the train to give certain kinds of information – and this role will enhance their authority. But equally every member of staff has a customer relations role (which involves communicating with words). So tone of voice is not a peripheral issue.

- **Make a commitment to being the leader in your industry in the use of words**

  To say that you will focus on tone of voice to improve customer relations is one thing. It is a far more radical decision to focus on it as a deliberate way of seizing the high ground and gaining competitive advantage. No one in the rail business has done it yet. You can.

Make it central to your brand.

- **Clarify the idea behind your tone of voice**
  It's too easy and too bland to say that we want a tone of voice that is friendly, accessible, informative etc. These are all good qualities but every company interested in customer service will be trying to develop a tone of voice which has those qualities.

You need to go further if you are to create some true differentiation for yourself

First you have to say that this really matters. You don't just pay lip service to these ideas but you commit yourself to achieving a real sense of difference. That sense of difference will come from there being an idea which is imbedded in the company – an idea of what you are really about, which will drive many of the things that you do as well as the way that you speak and write them.

Let's try to define something of that idea, using your own words from the Annual Report, as a starting point:

'Anglia Railways' train services are part of the fabric of East Anglia. We wish to play a key role in local development, working with the people and communities we serve to encourage train travel and increase prosperity in the region.'

In other words, you are more than just a train company. You are not just the rolling stock and the people who get you from Norwich to London and back. Of course you want to encourage use of your product – train travel – but there's an aim behind this which is to do with enriching lives.

This ties in with the essential advantages of train travel discussed earlier. We can express this as 'people on trains have more time to think, time to write, time to read, time to talk – and, if they wish, time to sleep'. You can say, as a result, that you are about helping people – your customers – make better use of their time.

And some of the vital ways in which people can use their time better is by developing their communication skills – or at the very least by having more time to practise them. Skills of reading, writing, talking – the use of language.

These skills can then be legitimately owned by you. There need be no strangeness in a railway company being committed to a belief in the value of language. Language is an enabler. It enables people to get more out of life, to make fuller use of their time, to play 'key roles in local development'.

There is a powerful idea there both for your customers and for your own people.

Find ways to express that idea – and constantly find new ways to keep expressing it

Let's define the idea as 'enabling people to get more out of life'. We do this through our product – train travel – which gives people more time to read, write, listen and talk.

The challenge is to find ways of expressing the strength and uniqueness of this idea through special things that we do.

A number of specific recommendations were made for 'special things' that Anglia could do.

Finally...

My main recommendation is to make it clear that you are focused on the value of words, that you enjoy words for all the different things they achieve and that this interest in words is a key component of your brand's personality.

A distinctive approach to language can then be as recognisable an element of your identity as colour. It can add value to all your communications and can itself drive specific initiatives.

End of report

As I said earlier, Anglia Railways was a cost-conscious operation. Many of the recommendations here were delayed or shelved, some were implemented. We ran tone of voice workshops with the customer service department. Andy Cooper moved to another train company. Many improvements were made but I remain convinced that the transport sector as a whole needs to make radical changes to the way it uses words. I suspect I am not the only rail traveller who believes that the change from talking about 'passengers' to 'customers' in the 1980s was a bit of a con. And when it comes to air travel, where it is phenomenally difficult to differentiate between brands through the in-flight environment (most airlines even use the same planes), there are wasted opportunities to give individual airlines more distinct personalities through the words that they speak and write. 'Singapore girl' at least raises expectations that you might receive different words as part of superior service. But why do so many airlines stick so relentlessly to the bland approach? Perhaps because they spend so much time in mid-Atlantic.

Anglian Railways had the distinct advantage, in terms of establishing a clear personality for itself, of being clearly defined by its geography. It could identify with its customers because they all came from the same region but inevitably this had the inbuilt danger that the company might seem parochial. This seems an ironic problem in a world where big companies are desperately keen to present themselves as 'global but local'. The next section deals with a global company, selling commodity products on the strength of individual care and relationships.

4 Generic engineering: Air Products

Selling air sounds a dubious proposition, yet some of
the world's biggest companies do just that. Air Products
and Chemicals Inc sells industrial gases and speciality
chemicals, and has its headquarters in Allentown,
Pennsylvania. Just down the road live the Amish, as
seen in the film *Witness*. It's a conservative part of
America and, on the face of it, an unlikely company to
have much truck with concepts like 'brand' and 'tone
of voice'. But, of course, unlike Anglia Railways, Air
Products cannot afford to be seen as parochial because it
operates in markets all around the world.

My first contact with Air Products came through
a meeting arranged at their UK offices near London.
The European communications director, John
Dodds, had brought together two of his colleagues to
talk to me about the company's 'global applications
development' (GAD) business. Colin Smith was English,
Cecil Chappelow was American; both of them were
engineers. Whatever I am, I am not an engineer.
They wanted me to write a brochure describing their
division of Air Products. It looked like it might be a
difficult meeting.

Perhaps it actually helped that I couldn't understand
any of the science. It forced them to talk to me about
what they actually did, which was to work closely
with customers to find new ways to use industrial
gases in manufacturing operations. There were stories
about people that made interesting listening. I had
a strong feeling that a 'brochure' would not do this
business justice, and through a proposal written after

the meeting I persuaded them to let me take a deeper look at the business and consider a more comprehensive communication programme.

This no doubt makes it all sound much easier than it was, but there was a refreshing openness in the approach taken by the Air Products people and a strong sense that I felt of their integrity. I had moved from a position of resistance to active engagement in the concerns of these genuine people. The proposal I wrote no doubt showed some of that conversion in my attitude. It is always easier to write convincingly if you have belief and enthusiasm for what you are writing. (And if you don't, you somehow need to conjure enthusiasm out of the act of writing.)

The outcome of this was that the GAD project was completed successfully. I had introduced them to a way of working, based on simply listening carefully to the concerns of a range of people, and they accepted this methodology completely. The recommendations I made – not for a brochure but for a series of communications based on the authority and knowledge of Air Products people – seemed to reveal to them a different way of thinking about themselves and what they did. The thinking was summarised in a bull's eye diagram.

John Dodds was particularly struck by possibilities of extending this kind of approach to the core business of Air Products. I was invited out to Allentown to meet people there and to see at first hand how the company operated at its centre. The same openness that I had encountered in the GAD people struck me again in Allentown. There was not necessarily a lot of sophistication in the company's approach to issues such as brand management, but there was a surprising willingness to learn. 'Our competitors BRAG. We don't.' This was a phrase that someone had spoken to me when talking about Air Products' approach. It became something of a mantra in every conversation. I could admire the refusal to brag but I couldn't accept that it was bragging to tell people about yourself. Air Products surely needed to communicate more, to tell the world that it was very good at what it did.

Through my work on GAD, I had defined the brand in that particular area of business. It happened to be an area that represented Air Products at its truest and best, and I had a feeling that the brand definitions could apply to the company as a whole. But, this being a company of engineers, there was a need to test these definitions almost to destruction. A major programme of research was embarked on, covering Air Products' own people, customers and potential customers, in the USA, Europe and Asia.

This was the biggest research programme I had been involved with and it was a great sign of trust that I was asked onto the team responsible for managing the programme. My role was to assess and to interpret the research, to translate the findings that were largely based on numbers into words that people could understand and act upon.

The research took many months to complete but at the end of it the whole team was able to agree on the conclusions. The research had assessed three 'brand propositions' which had emerged from internal focus groups and from my work on GAD. Each proposition was considered plausible by the team, and each proposition was then tested with customers and potential customers. The preferred proposition was the one that had greatest appeal to customers and also matched customers' view of the truth about Air Products; it was also very close to the one I had originally formed for GAD.

We were then asked to show what this really meant when it was translated into creative work for Air Products to communicate more effectively with many different audiences – customers, stock market analysts, local communities, employees, suppliers. We produced a number of different guidelines, including the one for tone of voice that follows.

Start of guidelines

Tone of voice

The definition of our brand makes demands of the way we speak and write when we represent our brand.

So we have to start with the brand positioning statement and brand values.

Our brand positioning

Brand positioning statement

Our strength is our great people. You can always recognise them by their understanding, integrity and passion. By aiming to deliver exceptional value, our people constantly strive for improvement – by listening, understanding and using their knowledge; by seeking ideas and making good ideas even better; by going the extra mile, often heroically. As a result, we create lasting relationships – always built on understanding.

Brand values

Understanding, Integrity, Passion

Our communications need to project clearly the brand positioning statement and values.

How can we embody these values in our communications? We need to think about the content of our communications and about the style.

Content

Our strength is our great people. We should demonstrate what we mean by this. The press and other stakeholder audiences are interested in the people who have been behind particular products, projects or programs. Use the human interest of our people.

Understanding is our dominant brand value. It means that we have to demonstrate ways in which we have used our understanding to develop projects, especially by working with customers. Probe into this when developing PR stories with Air Products people. Explore the possibilities of using real stories in case studies in preference to overblown description – let the facts of stories speak for us.

At the same time we need to show understanding of the needs of our immediate audiences in the media – we should think hard about how to meet those needs in the information we provide. Make it short, sharp and engaging, with real examples that can be used. Understand that this information will be used only if we make it interesting enough to use. And understand that our customers and other stakeholders will only read the material if we have related our writing to their interests.

Integrity is our second value. We have to be as honest and open as possible in what we say to people with whom we communicate, while maintaining our commercial interests. We should start from an expectation that it will be reasonable to give information rather than to withhold it.

Passion is our third value. We should seek ways to show that passion, by featuring people who are enthusiastic about what they do and by making clear that achievements are the result of inspired work by dedicated people.

Our commitments to stakeholders

We aim for complete honesty in relationships

We put great effort into communicating clearly about technology

We celebrate the achievements of our people

We anticipate customer needs with innovative products

We push quality standards higher and higher involving customers and suppliers

When we say something we do it

Our best practice operates wherever we operate in the world

We seek and share knowledge

How it makes me feel as a stakeholder

They settle only for what's best for customers

They value their own people and their relationships

They support me in my aims

I can trust them

They give me 100%

They're interested in me

The add value, they give me more

They speak my language

Our aim
To settle only for what's best for our customers both in terms of technology and value

Our essence
Last relationships built on understanding

Knowledge
Relationships
Honesty
Commitment

Determination
Dedication
Enthusiasm
Openness

Substantiators

Our characteristics
Understanding, integrity and passion

Written style

Our written style has to follow the same principles of the brand. The written word is a vital ingredient of our communications, and we should try to ensure that we express 'understanding, integrity and passion' through the way that we use language.

Because our values include understanding, our written style needs to be flexible to meet the needs of different audiences. For example, see the page on tone of voice in the *Advertising* section of these guidelines. The written style of advertising will be very different from the style of, say, a press release or a product data sheet or an academic research paper. But in each case we should try to express our brand values within the context created by the particular target readership for the communication.

Bear in mind that the first principle of writing is always to remember that there is a reader looking over your shoulder. This means asking yourself constantly: Have I communicated that message well enough? Think of what the reader wants, and modify the written style to meet readers' needs.

The brand values 'understanding, integrity and passion' mean that:

We should avoid using language that creates barriers to understanding by being too technical or jargon-ridden.

We should not use language that undermines our integrity by being too pushy and hard sell.

We should beware of language that fails to express passion by being boring and flat.

Because our brand is about people there should always be a strongly personal, individual feel to the written style. We should, wherever possible, use real people in the copy we write because the achievements of people represent what we stand for as a company. It follows that we should use people's own words as direct quotations, and that the overall tone of our written style should be close to the spoken word.

Write as if you were speaking.
Write as if you were telling a story.
But tell the story well.

Use the following checklist to assess whether you are achieving the right tone of voice. If you answer 'yes' to each question, you've got it right.

Understanding
Do the words create a sense of recognition and empathy through the human story?

Is the language direct and uncomplicated, suitable for the needs of the target reader?

Integrity
Do the words engage people with honest yet thoughtful writing?

Does the writing allow people's achievements to speak for the product or project?

Passion
Does the writing talk to the reader, as if in a conversation?

Does the writing sound as if it comes from an individual not from an anonymous corporation?

Overall, does it make you think 'tell me more'?

Tell me more
We should always aim for writing that meets these criteria and still leave people wanting to know more. By being clear that there are tangible benefits to dealing with us, as well as the likelihood of a relationship founded upon understanding of the customer's needs, we encourage the reader to want to find out more.

End of guidelines

There are general principles of writing described in the guidelines that might be thought applicable to many companies. That is true, but the particular executions that emerge from applying these guidelines to Air Products' own business are individual to the company.

Such communications exemplify the brand's values, embodied in the person writing the words, which are influenced by the target audience. We, me, them and it. What then emerges should be individual to Air Products and capable of truthful imitation by no one else.

The guidelines were completed in the summer of 1999. They were then put on hold as news began to unfold of a massive and complex merger / acquisition involving three of the four biggest players in the industrial gases market worldwide. Under the proposed deal Air Liquide and Air Products would acquire different parts of BOC. In the meantime, to the great benefit of the programme, John Dodds had been promoted to a role of champion of the brand, working in Allentown.

In the event, the deal proved too complicated and too difficult for the US competition authorities to accept. The plug was pulled on the merger in May 2000 but, in the meantime, we had been working to provide a range of communications, for people inside and outside the company, which would express the definitions of the Air Products brand agreed over many months.

As it always should be, the internal audience was considered to be vital. Printed and electronic materials, and a video, were produced. For external audiences new advertising appeared, based on the brand principles agreed a year earlier, and featuring the 'tell me more' strapline. It was a longer and more tortuous route that we had envisaged but, in the end, we arrived. Having arrived, we now need to think about how we move on. There's always the need to move on.

5 Fighting fires with words: Cable & Wireless

In the autumn of 1996 we were working happily with Bell Cable Media, developing a brand that was going to be called 'oneline'. The name reflected the company's strategy of integrating television, telephone and Internet services through one supplier and one cable into the home. This was an idea directed mainly at the residential market in the days before such integration became a reality.

Everything changed for us when Cable & Wireless stitched together a deal that brought three UK cable operators – Bell Cable Media, Videotron and Nynex – into its fold. This was a bit of a blow to us because we had become rather attached to our work on 'oneline' and now, suddenly, everything was up in the air.

It soon emerged that 'oneline' was dead. The reality of the power game that was being played was that Cable & Wireless was the conqueror. The acquired companies had to submit, and the people in them had to jostle for position and jobs. All we could do was back our Bell Cable Media clients and hope that they would emerge in positions of influence.

We were very lucky in the way that things worked out. A strategy group was set up to look at the question of the new brand that would represent Cable & Wireless Communications – i.e. the new company that was growing out of the ashes of the previous companies, including Cable & Wireless plc's best-known brand Mercury. All the previous brands were being killed off, to be replaced by the Cable & Wireless masterbrand. The strategy group included marketing representatives from each of the acquired (now defunct) brands, plus myself.

It was a strange situation. Marketing managers sat down to cooperate with counterparts who had weeks before competed against each other in the marketplace – and, in the weeks to come, would compete against each other for jobs. It was clear that the new Cable & Wireless Communications would severely reduce numbers employed. Out of ten people from the new company sitting around the table, perhaps only two would emerge with jobs.

It happened that these two people were Ruth Blakemore, appointed marketing director, and John Aarons, brand manager. They had been our main clients at Bell Cable Media and now, with them, we had the chance to create this new brand.

The idea was to use the solidity and credibility of the Cable & Wireless name – qualities needed in a marketplace which distrusted 'cable cowboys' – but to make the Cable & Wireless brand much more consumer-friendly than it had ever been before. Cable & Wireless plc would remain the corporate brand, facing the City. Ours would be the brand underneath that, appealing to cable customers in residential areas.

It was an intensive programme. As we worked on it, we sometimes felt that we were the only constant features because our 'clients' would disappear from their jobs overnight. A new chief executive, Graham Wallace, arrived as the launch day approached. A big advertising campaign (by Rapier) appeared on TV and in the papers, featuring a heavy use of yellow. The advertising was successful in achieving high levels of recognition for the new brand. The only problem was that behind the brand very little was actually working properly. There simply had not been enough time to bring together all the disparate operations into one smoothly running business. The work we were doing on the brand was papering over the cracks but ordinary customers were acutely aware that the cracks were real and deep.

We created comprehensive guidelines for the new brand. The visual idea was based on trying to make a virtue out of the problem posed by the Cable & Wireless symbol. This digitised version of the globe (known internally as the 'Death Star') had originally been designed years before when a merger with AT&T (globe symbol) seemed probable. The logic of creating two such similar symbols is still hard to understand. However, it seemed that we were now stuck with it because Graham Wallace would not contemplate changing it. So we created a visual system based on circles, echoing the globe symbol, but using playful images in the circles. These circular images then had a fixed visual relationship to the symbol – like the earth and moon. A comprehensive collection of guideline documents – ranging from promotional items to advertising to naming principles – was then produced.

We decided that one of these documents should be on tone of voice. We knew that there were terrible problems with customer service as the new company settled down. None of the four companies in their previous incarnations had been regarded as leaders in customer service – and now with the problems of rapid integration, things were certainly not improving on that front. The tone of voice document was intended primarily for people in customer services – those having to speak to customers on the phone, answer letters (mainly of complaint) and write proposals for new business. It seemed to us better to use the new brand to help in this situation than to bury our heads and hope the problems would blow away.

Start of document

We have a strategic vision – to lead the world in integrated communications

These are some of the things we have to do to turn that vision into reality:

- *Make sure that we deliver the benefits of technology to our customers and make it easy for them to use.*

- *Commit ourselves to the highest standards of customer service.*

- *Ensure that our approach is driven by understanding our customer needs, not by the desire to impose our own needs.*

- *Realise that the way we behave and the personality we present comes from within ourselves and affects our communication with others.*

These thoughts and actions have far-reaching implications for our business. The most important is that we will find it easier to achieve our strategic vision if we communicate in a style that matches our strategy.

In other words, we need to show our commitment to understanding customer needs in everything we do and say. If we want to make technology easy to use, we have to make efforts to explain technology in language that customers will easily understand. We have to show that we are listening well, and not fall back onto inappropriate ways of speaking and writing which suggest we are not listening well enough.

These guidelines are about 'tone of voice'. But tone of voice is not just a matter of writing style. It's about the way we do business, and we want people to enjoy the experience of doing business with us. We need to apply the same principles to the way we relate to each other, because each of us represents our brand. Words matter. They have a profound effect on the way people think about us. We should always try, with the words that we use, to leave a good impression.

'Often it is true that one picture is worth ten thousand words. But not necessarily worth one word. The right word.'

Bill Marsteller

We are not going to attempt to give guidance on the right words to use in any given situation. That would be impossible.

We will try, though, to give guidance on a few key areas that affect our business deeply. Let's start with writing letters to our customers, taking examples from existing letters. The examples used will show that we can improve the written style of our letters. We need to do this not simply to improve the style but to create a better relationship with customers that will build loyalty, trust and liking. They will also show that we have a great opportunity to be much more individual in our written style and to get more enjoyment from our approach.

For example...

Writing letters

Sometimes in our letters we can appear defensive and negative:

'The location of the cabinet follows our guidelines. The cabinet must therefore remain in its present location'

We can seem impersonal and bureaucratic:

'Your order will be processed'

'Your installation is scheduled for'

And sometimes we seem to be using words in a deliberate attempt to avoid being clear and straightforward:

'Our records indicate a potential service availability problem'

Often it is easy to use clichéd adjectives and phrases:

'We have a tailored range of highly competitive tariffs'

'Thank you' is the key thing we should say to our customers. Many of our current letters adopt a slightly insincere tone of voice. If we are too humble, however, in our attempt to show how committed we are to customer service, our customers will not trust us.

'I would like to thank you for your continued good custom'

'We thank you for your valued subscription'

All these phrases can be expressed more simply and in words that customers can relate to more easily. The first rule of letter-writing should be to write as if you are speaking — there should not be a big difference between the written and the spoken word.

So if you were speaking you might say:

'I'm delighted that you have decided to carry on using our service. Thank you for ringing to let us know.'

rather than

'Following your recent phone call to our customer service department, I was pleased to hear that you have decided to continue to use our service.'

It helps if we think carefully about every word and consider whether there's a simpler alternative.

For example, here are some words and phrases in current use in our letters alongside recommended alternatives.

telephony service	**telephone**
assist	**help**
upon receipt of	**when I receive**
commence	**begin**

permit	**let**
terminate	**end**
concerning	**about**
regarding	**about**
re	**about**

Companies still use the tired, old language of office-speak to express the simplest thoughts – such as 'about'. We should always try to avoid the impression that we are old-fashioned or bureaucratic – and make sure that we genuinely are not. (And, by the way, 'about' in a different meaning is better than 'approximately' – it is much less pompous.)

In general we should not have separate tones of voice for business and residential customers. In each case, remember that you are talking to an individual – you are having a conversation. Direct mail letters, however, have their own demands; we should never use direct mail techniques (like internal headings in letters) when writing to existing customers.

We should, however, always try to be positive and clear in what we write. Try to put the most positive thought first in a sentence. Avoid starting sentences with words that invite a cynical reply – e.g. 'Since we value our customers...'

As another point of guidance, try to be active and personal in your writing style. Write

'I will make an appointment'

rather than

'An appointment will be scheduled'

You are in control, not some mysterious and anonymous department.

Words are tricky. They can often mean different things to different people.

If we say the wrong words we might mislead, confuse or turn off a customer. It's always worth thinking about the right words to use – they will have a big influence on whether people like us or not, whether people buy from us or not.

Our launch advertising set the tone for the way we mean to go. By asking 'What can we do for you?' we showed that we are a company interested in others, not wanting just to sell what we make. If we really are interested in the needs and the lives of our customers, we should really try to follow this through into every dealing we have with customers.

Letters are an important interface between us and our customers. Sometimes they inform or explain, sometimes they say sorry, sometimes they sell. A more direct selling relationship needs a selling document – a proposal.

Writing proposals

Good writing is essentially about making sure your readers get the message you intended them to. Obvious, perhaps; but it does mean that to maximise your proposal's chance of success you need to pay attention to style as well as content.

Keep it simple

This section outlines a few principles which apply to writing in general, and especially to the writing of complex information. People writing this kind of material often use a style which they presumably think will make them sound educated, professional or clever; in effect, they sound merely pompous. Keep your style simple, and your message will be much clearer.

You will often need to use long words when you write about telecommunications; many have no shorter equivalent. However, try not to use long words where shorter ones would do just as well. By using them only when they are needed, you will increase their impact. And avoid 'pompous' words altogether. Some of these and their alternatives were listed in the section on 'writing letters' – here are some more.

Instead of this	would this do?
approximately	**about**
sufficient	**enough**

utilise	**use**
meet together	**meet**
on occasion	**sometimes**
commonly	**often**
frequently	**often**
is able to	**can**
is dependent upon	**depends on**
prior to	**before**
in excess of	**more than**
methodology	**method**
purchase	**buy**
transportation	**transport**
additionally	**and** or **also**
whilst	**while**
amongst	**among**
in close proximity to	**near**
situated near	**near**
commencement	**start**
firstly	**first**
we will take appropriate action	**we will do it**

Keep it correct

Some words are often misused. Try to watch out for them – your readers will not necessarily know what you mean, even if the wrong usage is a common one, and you will appear less credible. This is particularly important if your readers' first language is not English; if they take you literally, they could receive the wrong message altogether. Here are some examples which might occur in a typical proposal:

- *Impact, as a verb, does not mean 'have an impact on', but 'press closely into' or 'compress'. So if you say that something will 'impact the delivery schedule', you are implying that it will shorten the schedule, when you probably mean just the opposite.*

  Use 'affect' (or, in this case, 'lengthen') instead.

- *Be careful with 'consist', which needs 'of' and 'comprise', which doesn't. Do not say:*

The network comprises of eight sites.

but one of the following:

The network comprises eight sites.
The network consists of eight sites.
There are eight sites on the network.

- *Alternative means 'such that one or the other may be chosen'; alternate means 'one after the other, in turn'. So talk about alternative routes if this is what you mean.*

- *If you say that there is synergy between two things (like companies), you mean that they work in combination, not that there is similarity between them or that they have a lot in common.*

Keep it active

Without going into too much grammatical detail, the most basic sequence in an English sentence is subject

– verb – object, for example:

The user selects the appropriate bandwidth.

This is known as the active voice. If we turn it round and use the passive voice, the focus shifts and the sentence becomes longer:

The appropriate bandwidth is selected by the user.

Many people overuse the passive voice when writing technical documents – perhaps because of the way we were taught to write up our experiments in school science. The result is text that sounds heavy, over-formal and boring. The active voice gives a simpler, more concise sentence with more direct impact.

For example:

Manual intervention by the user will be necessary to clear the call.

is much more clearly expressed as:

The user must clear the call manually.

(This, of course, is also an example of removing long and pompous words.)

The best rule is:

Use the active voice unless you have a really good reason to prefer the passive.

Keep thinking

Long, convoluted sentences are disorienting for your readers, who may lose the thread of what you were saying before they reach the end. If they have to keep backtracking, they may well give up trying to read the sentence altogether.

Try breaking long sentences down to shorter ones. A good rule of thumb is to stick to one idea per sentence, and avoid sentences that run over more than three lines. However, this is not an unbreakable rule – too many very short sentences can give your writing a jerky 'staccato' feeling, making it unpleasant to read. Your writing will have a better flow and rhythm if you vary the length of your sentences.

Breaking your text into paragraphs makes it easier to read. In general, a paragraph should be used for each different 'idea' or statement.

Like the sentences in your document, the paragraphs should vary in length. But do try to keep them relatively short – a rule of thumb is: not more than two or three sentences and not more than seven or eight lines.

The occasional single-sentence paragraph can give impact to an important statement.

If you find that a paragraph is getting too long because the idea contained in it is complicated, consider how you could break it up – perhaps with a bulleted list, a table or a simple diagram.

'I'm a lousy copywriter, but I am a good editor. So I go to work editing my own draft. After four or five editings, it looks good enough to show to the client.'

David Ogilvy

Working with words

Our brand comes to life whenever we communicate – whether with each other, our customers or other audiences. We should always reflect our values when we communicate.

This means that everything we communicate should be both visually inspiring and written in a way which creates a personal relationship with our customers and each other. This will build trust and open opportunities for long-lasting relationships.

When you are writing anything on behalf of the company, just ask yourself: Are you using the kind of language you would be happy to read aloud?

If the answer is yes, what you write will be *credible*.

People will believe you.

If the answer is no, perhaps you are using language that sounds defensive or negative. People will not believe you.

Are you making an effort to avoid words that are complicated or technical?

If the answer is yes, your writing will be *accessible*.

If the answer is no, ask yourself whether you could write more simply without losing meaning.

Otherwise, if your readers know less than you know about the subject, they may not understand you.

Do your words sound as if they were coming from a responsive human being? If the answer is yes, Cable & Wireless will sound like a very *flexible* company.

If the answer is no, the company will come across as a faceless organisation.

Are you addressing your words from one individual to another?

If the answer is yes, you will sound real and *personal*.

If the answer is no, the company will appear cold and uncaring.

Are you telling people something new, in a different way? If the answer is yes, what you write will be *inspiring* for your readers.

If the answer is no, how do you hope to uplift the customer if you yourself are not uplifting?

Words express a personality. They say a lot about us. We should use them with respect and with enjoyment because they can help us to achieve so much.

End of document

The tone of voice document for Cable & Wireless was written to take account of the customer perspective. Disgruntled, angry customers seize on insensitive language to fan the flames of their own discontent. We were in a fire-fighting situation and the document helped to control the fire. But the fire continued because Cable & Wireless never really came to terms with the residential market for cable – it did not have much empathy with a large part of its expanded customer base, and it had lost many of the people who had customer service skills. Such is the way with restructuring and (dreadful, dreaded word) natural wastage. In 1999 Cable & Wireless decided to sell its residential cable interests and concentrate on the business market where it had originally made its name.

The lesson I would draw from this is not that the work failed but that it was never given a chance to succeed. A brand programme and, within this, a tone of voice programme, need commitment. There is no point in hoping that a short, sharp burst will fix things permanently. You will need persistence and you will need to keep renewing belief as people slip back into old ways, as new people come into your company wanting knowledge of your expectations of them. Belief and knowledge have to be supplied by those in the company who are champions of the brand – at the most senior level and right the way through the company. Everyone needs to feel that they are, to some extent at least, responsible for maintaining the brand and its tone of voice. But there are no rules for doing this.

The only rule I advocate is that there should be no real rule. Like the Nordstrom advice: 'Rule 1 is to use your own initiative.

There are no other rules.' Many books on writing start from the assumption that there are rules to be taught – follow the rules and learn to write. But writing is not like that. I simply suggest that you plunge in without being intimidated by the thought of rules. Only begin. And, having begun, keep on.

eep on keep on keep on keep on keep on keep on keep on keep on keep on kee

4T
TELLING
STORIES

'The thing about a book is that the man who is writing it brings all the lines from all the different places and makes them flow together in the same stream.'

Timothy O'Grady, *I Could Read the Sky*

1 A fresh perspective

In the previous chapters I looked at writing from the perspective of different parties involved in the shaping of the words that are used in business communications. This chapter is about the message itself, the stories we have to tell, but also inevitably about the way that we tell these stories.

My colleague Mark Griffiths responded to my diagram of 'we, me, them & it' with a diagram that he had been thinking about independently. The two diagrams are actually very close in spirit and in meaning, but I think Mark's is actually better suited to what I need to explore in this chapter. This is the diagram:

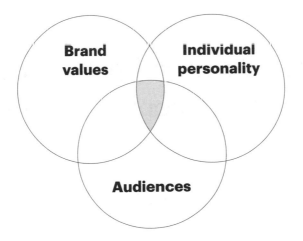

The shaded area at the heart of the diagram represents a brand's tone of voice. Only by bringing all parts of the diagram together in balance is it possible to achieve a distinctive and sustainable tone of voice. The diagram is simply another way of reaching for a truth. So, to explore this, we have to step lightly through some of the places we have already been so that we can look at them with fresh eyes.

2 Tying yourself down

Writers grapple with identity every time they write. I explored the relationships of language and identity in the first chapter which I called 'The trouble with words', a phrase taken from an interview with Dennis Potter. Partly because I admire him so much as a writer, partly because I now think of this association as a kind of talisman, I'm going to use some more words by Dennis Potter as a starting point for my argument.

'I'm a writer: I put words in other people's mouths.'

Dennis Potter, *Cold Lazarus*

That's the apparent advantage of being a writer. It seems to give you some influence over the words that go in mouths and over whose mouths you put words in. Sometimes it's a matter of putting words into the mouth of a company, and that's the kind of writing which is the main focus of this book's attention. This makes it all the more important to think of the company as a person – or at least as a collection of people.

Words matter to me because they can do so much. They convey information and they display emotion. They talk, they sing, they dance, they walk. More than anything else they give pleasure.

It was good to see the sheer fun of words employed so well by Will Awdry in the 1997 D&AD material.

1997 British Design & Art Direction

Welcome to Descriptions, pet. Rain or shine, us words are always right busy. Precision work. Proud to do it, chuck. Fr'instance, this one here says **D&AD Showreel Index**. Left to Bragging, it would be a video shop by now. Mind, there are some who wouldn't touch it. Received Pronunciation won't show for less than a shipping forecast these days. Hoity-toity lot. Though a sight better than those common little sluts up in Vernacular. Drop their aitches for anyone, they will. And Franglais! Brassy French tarts flashing their circumflexes. Disgusting, it is. **35**

One of my earliest memories of the association between language and pleasure is of reading the label on the HP Sauce bottle. Even without understanding French at the time there was something magical in the words

LA SAUCE HP
ENTIÈREMENT NATUREL.
UN MÉLANGE DE HAUTE
QUALITÉ DE FRUITS
ORIENTAUX, D'ÉPICES ET
DE VINAIGRE.

On the other side of the label was the English version so you could work out something of what it meant.

HP SAUCE
MADE FROM A SECRET RECIPE,
BLENDING A SPECIAL SELECTION
OF THE WORLD'S FINEST
TOMATOES, DATES AND SPICES WITH
MALT VINEGAR NATURALLY MATURED
IN WOODEN VATS AND WATER
FROM HP'S OWN WELL.

Language expresses what we think. It also shapes the way we think. However, much as I believe in words, I believe more in the power of words and images in combination. Let me give you a light-hearted example first. On the next page is a postcard that I sent home to my son and daughter one summer when I was holidaying with my wife in Tuscany. The image was chosen from postcards on the rack, but it suggested these words to me.

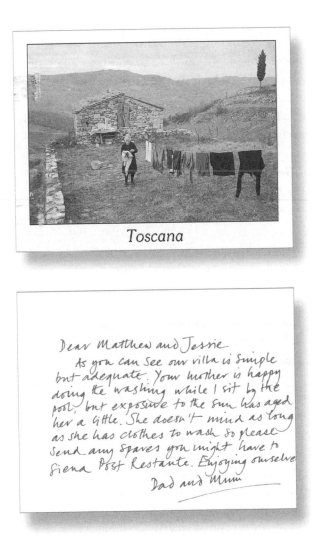

Toscana

Dear Matthew and Jessie.

As you can see our villa is simple but adequate. Your mother is happy doing the washing while I sit by the pool, but exposure to the sun has aged her a little. She doesn't mind as long as she has clothes to wash so please send any spares you might have to Siena Post Restante. Enjoying ourselve

Dad and Mum

In that case it was good to have the discipline of a postcard. We perceive words differently when we see them in different settings. Words are infinitely flexible and they respond to being prodded, trimmed and shaped by their surroundings. Sometimes sheep, sometimes shepherds, one word can lead to another. The visual environment in which words exist can also lead you down unexpected paths. Douglas R Hofstadter wrote, in a book that is 500 pages of exquisite words about translation:

'The amount of influence exerted on my text by concerns of purely visual esthetics is incalculable –

and by "my text" I don't merely mean how I wound up phrasing my ideas, I mean the ideas themselves...

I suspect that the welcoming of constraints is, at bottom, the deepest secret of creativity.'
Douglas R Hofstadter, *Le Ton beau de Marot*

Hofstadter was thinking particularly of constraints imposed by translation and poetry. No form of writing has more constraints than poetry, but it was extraordinary when poets like George Herbert demanded that the visual form of the poem should also be used to shape and express the meaning of the words. *Easter-Wings* has the shape both of a bird's wings (the dove that is the holy spirit) and of spiralling flight. The words then respond to the thoughts suggested by this form.

Easter-Wings
George Herbert

Lord, who createdst man in wealth and store,
Though foolishly he lost the same,
Decaying more and more,
Till he became
Most poore:
With thee
O let me rise
As larks, harmoniously,
And sing this day thy victories:
Then shall the fall further the flight in me.

My tender age in sorrow did beginne:
And still with sicknesses and shame
Thou didst so punish sinne,
That I became
Most thinne.
With thee
Let me combine
And feel this day thy victorie:
For, if I imp my wing on thine,
Affliction shall advance the flight in me.

You have to love the constraints. In the case of
writing as part of corporate identity you are rightly
constrained by what is appropriate for the company and
the people in it. You understand those constraints only
if you have immersed yourself in the company for which
you are writing.

Unfortunately, much thinking on corporate identity has revolved around the need to present a corporation's power. Military analogies abound. Flags are placed strategically around the global map and these flags symbolise global power. But is this vision of empire enough? Should this idea of corporate identity – often described as the 'most powerful of strategic business weapons' – be placed at the disposal only of the already mighty? And, even if so, does it have to be used to make the mighty look even mightier? I wonder if we all share this admiration for the right of might or will we want to side with the guerrilla forces?

Such visual identities of course come with their verbal equivalents, talking inevitably of the need for uniformity rather than diversity. The biggest problem is that companies want safety and they want to avoid the taking of risks. It's easy to be safe with words. They bring their own security, particularly when you wrap yourself in familiar ones. The easy thing is to talk about quality and service and putting customers first – it's easy and safe because people recognise the words and what they are supposed to stand for. But do you mean something better than that, something that makes your company special?

There is lip-service paid to flexibility and to keeping options open but the reality is that the range of options is kept narrow. Like the former Colonial Minister visiting Africa in the 1960s, we venture out with a sunshade in one hand and an umbrella in the other. We hate to be caught out, we hate to make mistakes, but the truth is that we only make progress if we take a chance and try to do something we haven't done before.

'It's strange that words don't have worse consequences than they do.'

Javier Marias, *A Heart So White*

When I used these words in tone of voice guidelines for Cable & Wireless someone objected that words do have terrible consequences. Perhaps it's an indication that I'm from the halffull rather than the half-empty state of mind but for me the sentence reads as an expression of the positive power of words. Words can have bad consequences, they can abuse and be abused, but so can other tools of our trade.

The example cited to me was of Hitler and it's interesting to be reminded that the Nazis too had verbal as well as visual elements in their identity. We think of the symbols, colours, torchlight processions and the grandiose architecture, and these were undoubtedly powerful as well as evil in their consequences. But we should also think of the sound of the Third Reich, the use of words that are familiar even to those who speak little German. You might imagine thousands of voices in unison chanting 'Sieg heil', 'Ein Volk, ein Führer'.

Clearly the identity of the Nazis encompassed language because it expressed their philosophy. The fact that they commandeered visual and verbal elements of the national identity – 'Deutschland über alles' – is something we need to consider when the debate rages over Britain's identity and the use of symbols like the Union Jack. If we think of the quintessentially American identity, the words 'the star spangled banner' are a potent signal to set beside the flag itself.

My point is that language has enormous power to influence minds and it is inextricably part of identity. But we recognise it as an element of identity less readily than we recognise logos, colours or typefaces.

> *'If the times are upside down, the language must be too. And, believe it or not, the choice of words and image is near the centre of business strategy.'*
> Tom Peters

If companies such as 3M have been saying that they are trying

> *'to sell more and more intellect and less and less materials'* …

If Microsoft says

> *'our only asset is the human imagination'*…

If International Thomson is trying

> *'to change the way the world learns'*…

It's clear that the competitive business environment is about out-thinking others in the marketplace. How do we think? Primarily we think with words. If we think well, we write well. If we write well, it's good evidence that we are thinking well.

Doesn't this mean that companies should give a lot more attention to the way they express their identities through words?

'Knowledge is useless unless you know how to communicate it – in writing.'

David Ogilvy, *The Unpublished David Ogilvy*

3 Setting yourself free

This could be mistaken for the teaching part of the book so let me add a disclaimer.

It seems to me that what you are taught to do is inherently less valuable than what you learn to do by your own discovery.

There's a big difference between believing something because you were told it, and believing something because you have experienced it. In a way it sounds like a complete abdication of responsibility for teaching. In fact I think it's the opposite because it places heavier demands on the 'teacher'. Learning depends on thinking your way past questions not on being given answers.

I also like Alan Bennett's thought about the National Gallery. He said there should be a notice hanging in it which says:

'You don't have to like everything here'

It's a good thought because we often strive too hard for an idea of perfection and, in the creative business perhaps more than in any other, we can be dismissive and absolute in our judgements. There is a fine line between obsession and integrity, between pride in our work and obstinacy. If you keep crossing the line you end up getting less pleasure from diversity and you miss out on a lot of the fun of words.

There's no doubt about the extraordinary diversity of the English language swirling and swelling before our eyes as fresh currents – from popular culture, other languages or English speakers from different countries – change its composition. I wrote these adverts to celebrate the evolution and diversity of English as a way of promoting the *Cambridge International Dictionary of English*.

If you want to learn English as it really is ... if you want to teach English as it really is ... there's only one sensible choice of dictionary.

The Cambridge International Dictionary of English (CIDE) contains a wealth of innovative features to help students understand and use English confidently and accurately.

Comprehensive
Clear
International

Wan.na.be *only Cambridge will guide you to the real meaning.*

Cambridge University Press,
ELT Marketing,
The Edinburgh Building,
Shaftesbury Road, Cambridge CB2 2RU, UK
Tel: (01223) 325819 Fax: (01223) 325984

WANNABE

🏛 **CAMBRIDGE**
UNIVERSITY PRESS

I'm always interested in starting points. It seems to me that the greatest problem we all have with writing is simply making a start. And to write commercially you need to get the point across fast.

I was amused when I visited Assisi to discover that Saint Bernard is the patron saint of advertising because his sermons were always 'clear, short and to the point'.

I also found out that Saint Clare is the patron saint of television. This is because she was able – although separated from him for most of their lives – to see and hear Saint Francis performing Christian services from a distance.

One of my first jobs was to write a summary of an official report on the management of agricultural grasslands in the UK. I started:

'Mention grass and most people think of a lawn...'

In those days we were less familiar with names for cannabis so the opening seemed to work because it established a tone that was different from the expected tone of an official report. And we should always try to challenge expectations but also to make sure, above all, that our message is read.

This is a compelling opening to a book even before you know who said it:

'My first memory is really the smell of the inside of my pram. It was plastic and the smell of the hood. Vivid memory. I was born at home not in hospital. The biggest disruption was when Mummy decided to leg it.'

edited by Andrew Morton, *Diana: Her True Story in her own Words*

When you know it's by Princess Diana, it's even more remarkable. The words are from the audio version. These are spoken words in a written form, but the energy of the written words comes from the flouting of the grammatical rules normally dictated by convention. Sentences need verbs. And so on.

It has always seemed to me unarguable that authors should pay enormous attention to the opening lines of their books. It also seems almost universally true that great books have great openings.

For the last few years I've been testing this theory because our identity for the Harvill Panthers imprint incorporates the opening lines of the book on each jacket. For me the use of those lines is the essential element of the Panther identity.

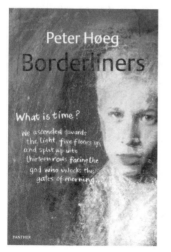

When we think of identity we think of names.
Of course names help define identity but they are not
always accurate in doing so. Big Daddy the wrestler
was christened Shirley and it's hard to believe that John
Wayne would have achieved success under his real name
Marion Morrison.

This looks apocryphal but I'm assured that this notice
posted in the southern states of the USA was genuine.
It was photographed by Susan Lippa. As for the dog in
question he obviously struggled to live up to the name,
but that's a common affliction.

LOST DOG
THREE LEGS.
BLIND IN LEFT EYE,
TAIL BROKEN.
MISSING RIGHT EAR
RECENTLY CASTRATED
ANSWERS TO NAME
"LUCKY"

Many company names are no more than obvious declarations of marketing intent. These names get invested with a totemistic power which they cannot bear in practice because the thought behind them is too shallow. A quick flip through the telephone directory uncovered the following:

GL⊕BALINK

MARKETPOWER

House of Art

World Access Europe

It's as well to remember my favourite Ron Atkinson story. When managing one of his many former football clubs, Ron was standing on the touchline as his striker got involved in a collision. The trainer ran onto the pitch to see to the player and reported back: 'He's concussed, doesn't know what his name is.'

Ron replied:

'Tell him he's Pele and send him back on'

My favourite company names are those that combine the visual and the verbal in an inevitable combination. Shell is one example. Another is the name I proposed to replace Trade & Travel Handbooks, the publisher of travel guides to places that are off the beaten track. As often I do, I thought of a story that related to the idea of the company, and the story was Robinson Crusoe coming upon evidence that someone else inhabited the island where he had been shipwrecked. The company now publishes as Footprint Handbooks.

It seems to me that there is often much more behind a name than first meets the eye – and that we sense this secret even if we don't know it. In other words there is a narrative that underlies a name, and the name is simply the title of that narrative. But it's the sense of depth that gives resonance to the name.

I sometimes try to turn this to a more deliberate advantage when inventing new names. For the Hot Bagel Company we invented a range of product names that were accompanied by snippets of stories written in a New York persona, somewhere between Damon Runyon and Woody Allen.

A sense of location is one of the essential elements of good writing. Think of any great writer – Dickens, Joyce, Patrick White, Fitzgerald, Steinbeck – and it's hard to separate them from the sense of place that they create through their writing. Take someone's mind out of the place where they are, put them somewhere else, vividly, and you create something more memorable than mere words.

SoHo Bagel
The people were all artists, or so they claimed.
But at least the bagels in SoHo were genuine works of art.

Brooklyn Bagel
Brooklyn Bridge and the Expressway were thick with automobiles.
But up on the Heights it was like another, quieter age.
Time enough to enjoy a bagel.

42nd Street Bagel
On 42nd Street everything is over the top.
It's gaudy, brash and a bit dangerous.
I made for the healthiest thing in sight.
I couldn't keep my hands off the bagels.

Liberty Bagel
I took the Staten Island ferry.
Manhattan was at my back, the Statue of Liberty on my right.
The wind was cold, but the bagel in my hand was hot.

Pizza Bagel
I walked away from Greenwich Village, and Little Italy smelt good.
The smell from the Pizza joint mingled with the bagels baking.
I thought 'How about if we put the two together?'

Broadway Bagel
On Broadway it's hard not to get dazzled by the lights
and the glitz. You need something to hold on to.
All I had was a bagel, but it was enough.

Fifth Avenue Bagel
Fifth Avenue is about as smart as you can get.
Even the crowds are chic, the bagels have style.

Empire Bagel
There was no denying it, the Empire State Building was huge.
I felt giddy looking at it. I had a bagel to keep things in proportion.

Second Avenue Bagel
I had my first bagel in Second Avenue. Then I had my second.
I wanted to make sure it really did taste good. It did.

The Holly and the Hare

That Christmas, snow came overnight and in the morning it glistened in the · wintry sunshine. Walking in the woods to gather holly, we came upon a hare. Startled, it looked me in the eye, then bounded away leaving small but deep footprints in the snow

Place is a vital element of story, but it is only one element. When WH Smith wanted me to think of names for different Christmas stationery ranges, I wrote three stories instead. The stories suggested the visual approach for each range and gave them a depth that names by themselves would have lacked. Peter Firmin's illustration provided its own sense of location.

We ascribe meanings to adjectives derived from people's names. Often these are writers we might have read. Somehow we know, or think we know, why a situation is Kafkaesque. We know what is Freudian even without reading Freud. How many of us have read Proust, yet we all have nibbled at the Proustian madeleine cake? In the twentieth century in particular we had a shared sense of a higher culture that we whittled down to a level we could more easily scale.

That's fine in itself but there's a danger in reducing everything to a form of words that is simply too thin. If you consciously restrict your vocabulary – and some companies do this – you end up with the linguistic equivalent of junk food, and you can all supply your own examples, not necessarily from the fast food business.

So by all means let's avoid jargon, let's aim to be clear, but let's not remove idiosyncrasy from language. Otherwise we'll have to resign in disgust like the tabloid journalist whose use of 'long words' like *marmalade* and *corrugated iron* were edited down to *jam* and *tin*. Plain English has its limits.

No doubt technology will test its limits in the coming years. Technology brings its own constraints and will therefore create new forms of language.

211

When I write or receive an e-mail, I'm aware that the style is different from that of a traditional letter. It's shorter, terser, straight to the point, and normally more informal, probably sloppier. In my case, that's partly because I type badly. In Nigel Coan's case, that's simply because he's Nigel.

Note for John Simmons
From: Nigel Coan
Date: Mon, Jun 2, 1997 10:34am
Subject: Printing Stuff
To: Communications, Packaging
DOWNSTAIRS FIERY
Don't print A3 cause it ain't bleeding working.
Print only A4 cause it is bleeding working.

It's good to invent new words. *Chortle* is a famous neologism, invented by Lewis Carroll, but who knows if we mean the same by it as he did? I state, purely to register it in public, that my personal contribution here is *architrove* which I define as an encyclopedia of architecture.

Shakespeare might be credited with creating more new English words than any other writer in history, but for me the excitement of Shakespeare derives from discovering layers of meaning in perfectly familiar words.

Patrick Spottiswoode of Shakespeare's Globe told me of the time when the Bishop of London, visiting the building while it was being constructed, said to him: 'We must remember our churches as you have remembered the Globe.' The reference there was to the

Ghost of Hamlet's father calling out 'Remember me!' Shakespeare, as usual, had at least two meanings in his head.

We must *remember* too – we must put bodies and people back into our work. We must remember the root meaning of corporate identity. What we have to do is help companies remember.

We can, if we choose, use words with this degree of respect. We can be conscious of words and the effect that they have, and we can certainly avoid being dishonest with words. **Downsizing**, for example, although ugly, is at least clinging by its fingernails to a notion of honesty. **Rightsizing** is downsizing with a dubious moral judgement.

Words betray our personalities. We make subjective judgements that derive from perception, taste or attitude, and these shape the way we write. 'It's a bit blowy today' or 'There's a nice breeze' – our personalities dictate the way we think and speak and write.

For example, are you by temperament a noun or an adjective or a verb person? Michael Wolff always tries to get companies to describe themselves by verbs. Instead of them saying, 'We're committed to quality', get them to say, 'We check everything'. It just means a little bit more.

He also gave me the wonderful example of two photocopiers made by different companies. When you turned them on in the morning, one said 'Ready', the other said 'Start'. Were these words chosen by pure chance or were they chosen to reflect different brand personalities through the use of a submissive adjective and a positive verb?

We have these building blocks of language and we use nouns, verbs and adjectives to make sentences.

Nouns are like buses – no use to anyone when they come along in threes. The first noun is overcrowded with meaning and you can't take it all in. Half your attention's taken by the second one. And the third one is just stuck behind, waiting to pull out and desperate to be first.

business improvement capability

network distribution management

Verbs are better when they're kept short. It suits their impulse to action.

Some people try to abolish adjectives as a quality control measure in business writing. That seems to me a terrible failure of imagination and trust. Trust in yourself to choose the right adjective.

We should not forget adverbs either because they have their own funny ways. I particularly look out for them when they take to the sports field with the double adverb *magnificently well* or the use of the adjective as adverb as in *he's bowling superb* or *the boy's done great.*

A more conscious verbal trick is to use lists, so that the resonance builds from the saying of each word.

'I have nothing to offer but blood, toil, tears and sweat.'

Winston Churchill

Or, as we might put it in the bullet point language of business:

'My offer:
- *Blood*
- *Toil*
- *Tears*
- *Sweat*'

Does that lose something in translation? Great words – particularly words that are at the emotional heart of a nation's identity – almost demand to be spoken and written with a flourish.

Politicians usually run only to sets of three words in combination. This popular device can be traced back to St Paul who showed the way with his epistle on Faith, Hope and Charity. The Steve Bell adaptation to put it into the language of Tony Blair was a modern and funny variant.

The device obviously works well and businesses have echoed it too with slogans like Marks & Spencer's 'Quality, Service, Value'. The individual words are fairly empty catch-alls, whose only memorable feature is the use of the three in combination.

Although brevity in writing is a virtue you can take it

too far.

A bridge too far. The bridge of sighs. Size is a virtue. Virtue is its own reward. One word leads to another, but don't feel the need to follow the compulsion to set down every sign down every turning into what might turn into culs-de-sac. Equally people believe that repetition is a vice, whereas it can be a useful stylistic device.

Can be.

Context is all. Take a simple phrase like 'As you will already know . . . ' and it's perfectly unremarkable. Put it in a situation where Kelvin Mackenzie, the editor of *The Sun*, writes a letter to sack the paper's astrologer and 'As you will already know' becomes very funny (if not to the recipient).

Ambiguity is never far away from the surface meaning of words in English. We have such a rich language that words are capable of many layers of meaning. We should use that to advantage when possible and we should be careful it doesn't work to our disadvantage by creating confusion.

Ambiguity can be dangerous. When Derek Bentley called out **'Let him have it, Chris'** it cost him his life because Christopher Craig shot the policeman instead of handing over the gun. Other examples are less life-threatening, although depressed sauce bottles might turn violent and machines might become alarmed if they miss last week's bargain (*see next page*).

There's a longer English history of deliberately not saying what you mean. There's a lovely word called *litotes* which means understatement, that is often used in descriptions of the oldest English poetry. Here I'm talking about English before it became anything like recognisable modern English – this is the Anglo-Saxon period that produced poems like *Beowulf*. When the Beowulf poet says, 'It was not far', he means that it was half a step away. This established a tradition where you give emphasis to something by underemphasis.

A modern variant of this is using a word that means the opposite of the real meaning – where bad means good, where wicked also means good, where *The half-decent football magazine* becomes a proclamation of quality, where *The Average White Band* is an underclaim we're no more to believe than that Carlsberg is *probably* the best lager in the world.

To prove that there is something peculiarly British in this characteristic, think of Captain Oates. I mean not just the famous last words, 'I'm just going out and may be some time', but the letter he wrote to his mother from Antarctica:

'The climate is very healthy although inclined to be cold.'

Captain Oates

I admire that kind of understatement, but I'm not sure how well it travels. I suspect it's one of those values which is actually at the heart of the real brand that is Britain. Speakers of American English don't appreciate it as readily although I believe there is a strong attachment to irony among American writers.

Just to demonstrate this, and to pave the way for more serious points about storytelling, there's the example from *Cheers* where Sam Malone compares one of his baseball performances to a Kamikaze. Woody, the

innocently dense barman, continues the conversation
with the words:

'Hey, I always wanted to meet one of those guys. The stories they must tell.'

4 Making the most of your freedom

Put all these ingredients of language together –
individual nouns, verbs, adjectives, adverbs, prepositions
– and you have an almost infinite menu of possibilities at
your service. Above all, you have the possibility to put
these combinations together to tell stories.

Aristotle wrote of story as the first requirement for
drama. Storytelling is fundamental to our culture –
not just our written culture – and is a hidden aspect of
corporate personality. I'm interested in story both from
the point of view of discovering the stories that reveal a
company's personality and of making them an enduring
part of a company's culture.

It's different when you're dealing with a brand-
new company. Barrington Stoke is the name for a
publisher of books for children with reading difficulties.
We decided on the name Barrington Stoke when I
heard that the two founders originally came from

villages called Barrington and Little Stoke. The name Barrington Stoke seemed right for a person rather than a place and suggested a story to me that would help to give the new company an instant history, that would explain its reason for being and that would guide it in future years. Here is the story of Barrington Stoke, as told in the company's literature.

The story goes that he would arrive at twilight, carrying a lantern to light his way and signal his arrival. In the village meeting place he set down his lantern and placed five stones in a circle around him. The young people of the village sat inside the stone circle while Barrington Stoke stood at the front in the light of his lantern. Each of the stones represented a subject for storytelling: adventure, mystery, fable, discovery and exploration.

He turned his lantern to shine on one of the stones and that decided the nature of the first story to be told: a story of exploration, for example. In the flickering light the children sat entranced while Barrington Stoke told the tale. And then another. And then another, until they were tired and ready for sleep. But Barrington Stoke's imagination was never exhausted – he moved on to the next day, the next village, the next story.

As with people, I think we come to like companies better if we start to know them through their stories, through the way that they talk about the things that they do and the things that matter to them.

When we were working with the life assurance company, the Prudential, we realised that they, perhaps more than any company in the UK, had a store of stories that they were simply not putting to any use. And, unfortunately, because this is a tale of personal failure, these are stories that they are still not using. I offer the idea now, as I offered it then, almost as a public service.

What we wanted to do with the Prudential was to publish a book of stories – or even do it on the Internet so that the project could constantly grow and be there as a therapeutic resource. The stories would be anecdotes and longer pieces by lots of ordinary people – the everyday customers of a life assurance company – about friends and relatives who had died. I had one real example, the memoir about his father written by a friend of mine for his children.

Put others alongside this and the stories (as such stories are) would be funny, compelling and moving.

We presented a challenge, of course, by raising a taboo subject. Is it corporate death to associate yourself with death? But let's not get silly and pretend that people don't die. That's the fact of life on which life assurance companies are based.

This is Geoff Dobson's story about his father, written for his children Tom and Dan.

I am writing to remember my father who died five months ago. Maybe his personality began to fade 12 years ago, when the first signs of Alzheimer's disease started to show. Even before that he was very polite and private. The disease strangely produced flashes of the spark that I had only occasionally experienced during my childhood. Unless I have forgotten.

The easiest memories are anecdotes shared with friends and loved ones to relieve the sorrow. Sorrow that drags on and on as the disease increases its hold. Finding humour provided some strength amid the tedium of tortured, obsessive and latterly aggressive behaviour.

About one year after Mum died Dad lost his free bus pass. I used to like to think he could do more than most observers would have believed. Perhaps I hoped that optimism would provide a magical force to reverse the inevitable decline. By 1986 it was in any event no longer clear to me whether some form of senility was the main problem. Reactive depression, the hopelessness he found without Vicky, could have produced the same effect.

Anyway, I sent him to the kiosk for his photos, required for the bus pass application form. Dad returned triumphant, the strip of four pictures clutched proudly, not remembering why but hanging on to the message.

Dan was ten at the time. Have you seen a child cry with laughter? – Not vindictively, but wonderfully overcome with complete surprise and engaging the subject, his grandpa, with the pure joy of the occasion. I began laughing before I reached them. Dan was holding the photos. Grandpa had lost the link with Dan and was happily stroking Beauty the dog. I had to prise Dan's hand open. Laughter can tighten the grip. Photos run in sequence top down.

It, telling stories

Illustration by Mac McIntosh

We, me, them & it

First came a lovely clear picture of a blue curtain. If the curtain had been brighter it might have been a David Hockney painting. It was a still photograph.

Second came the back of Dad's head, stretching diagonally across and upwards, shoulders thrusting into view. He was facing the blue curtain.

Third came Dad's startled face, very close. He must have turned round very quickly, alarmed by the flash. Head and shoulders were still leaning across and upwards. Eyes were open wide and behind his oldest pair of spectacles. The gaps around his false teeth could be seen. His face was bright, alarmed by the light.

Fourth and last came the seated pose. Dad could still move quickly if a simple clear message reached his brain. It would, however, have taken another dozen or so pictures to realise the need for the head to be at a certain level, let alone fathom the mechanics of an adjustable swivel seat. So, we had our picture. Dad's head was at the top. His silver hair had been cut off, but he could still be recognised. No doubt about it, that was Dad, as any bus conductor would be able to see.

As Dan's energy faded Dad began to sense that he had brought happiness to the world. He produced his party trick. His top set of teeth dropped down leaving his one peg on show. Then, swallow, and the bottom set joined the top ones under his top lip revealing two more brown pegs. Happy with life he took Beauty for a walk round the block. Dan went too. The photo strip was on the table. I wish I knew where it is now.

The idea for the book was actually all about the celebration of life. We live for a span, and while we're here we try to make an impression on the people around us. If they remember us and tell stories about us and the things that we did in our lives, it means that we've had a real purpose in living. So my idea was to encourage that kind of storytelling and associate the Pru with it.

It didn't happen because they decided instead to publish a history book to commemorate 150 years in business. Notions of storytelling are not the stuff of standard management text books so it's not easy to persuade companies to embrace them.

I'll give you another example and, again, I want to be honest so I cannot claim it as a triumph. We were working with an Indian company called Hero Motors. We thought that Hero was a great name, so how had it come about? The answer, disappointingly, was that they had bought the company and the name 40 years earlier and no one now knew why it had been called Hero. So we felt that a story was needed to explain the name. This is the story.

The story of Arjuna

*In the Mahabarata we read the story of the Pandavas,
the five brothers who became great heroes. As young men
they were taught everything that princes might be expected
to know but, of course, they all had different strengths
and weaknesses.*

*One day an archer was teaching them to use the bow and
arrow. They went out into a field and the archer invited the
brothers one by one to step forward and take up the bow.*

*'See that tree,' said the archer to the first brother. 'Tell me
what you see there.'*

*The first brother said: 'I see the tree. It has branches and
leaves. There is a bird sitting on a branch.'*

'Then do not shoot, do not shoot.'

*The second, third and fourth brothers came forward one
after the other, took up the bow and arrow and each said:
'I see the tree. It has branches and leaves. There is a bird
sitting on a branch.' Dissatisfied with the answers the archer
would not let them shoot.*

'Tell me what you see, Arjuna.'

*Arjuna stepped forward, drew back the string of the bow,
looked along the arrow and said: 'I see the head of a bird.'*

'Then shoot, Arjuna, shoot.'

The problem was that the story made the management of the company slightly uneasy. Indians in an Indian company striving to be a twenty-first century multinational felt uncomfortable with something that seemed to hark back to traditional, ethnic roots. In the event, we used the story to develop the company's visual identity and Arjuna the archer features in the company's new logo. In time I hope the story will be used to develop the company's legend.

We all need legends, companies too. Some years ago WH Smith started to talk about 'legendary customer service'. The problem was that it did not have enough stories of outstanding customer service to create legends. You need to do more than talk about legends, you need to live them.

It's said that there is only a handful of basic stories in the world. Through our educational work for Royal Mail we have been able to develop ideas on mythology and narrative that derive from the Canadian literary critic Northrop Frye. The contention is that myths are the basis for all storytelling, and that these archetypal stories relate to and reflect the natural cycle. The myths of spring, of dawning and birth, defeating the powers of darkness, winter and death, represent the archetype of romance. The Greek myth of Persephone is an example.

Winter into Spring

This myth comes from Ancient Greece and tells the story of Persephone, the daughter of Demeter, the goddess of the harvest.

In the days when gods and goddesses walked on the Earth, the three most powerful gods were brothers. Zeus was ruler of the sky. Poseidon was god of the sea and Hades was lord of the underworld.

The underworld was a terrible place, a place without light, where the spirits of the dead went. Having entered the underworld, and having eaten there, no one was allowed to re-enter the world of the living.

A beautiful girl lived on the Earth and her name was Persephone. One day Hades visited Earth and rode past Persephone while she was gathering flowers in a field. He was dazzled by her beauty. He wanted her.

And being one of the three most powerful gods, he kidnapped her and drove off in his chariot.

Persephone was terrified. She was pinned to the floor of Hades' chariot while he drove faster and faster, down and down, into the darkness of the underworld. In the black halls of Hades, Persephone crouched and cried, refusing all food, refusing to speak to the god who had snatched her away.

Days passed. Persephone's hunger grew. At last she could resist no longer, she ate some pomegranate seeds and, having eaten, she could not return to the world above.

Meanwhile her mother, the goddess Demeter, grew distracted. She knew what had happened but she could do nothing. She raged all the more because she was powerless against Hades.

She went to Zeus, the king of gods, and she begged him to bring about Persephone's return. Zeus could not bear Demeter's crying. Her tears were destroying the harvest. He had to do something.

Unfortunately he was too late to stop Persephone eating the pomegranate. The rules of the underworld had to be obeyed. Yet, Zeus being Zeus, the rules could be stretched a little. He sent Hermes, the messenger of the gods, to strike a deal with Hades. The deal was this. Persephone would marry Hades and remain Queen of the underworld, living there half the year. In the Spring she could return to Earth, and live there in the warm, bright light of the Summer. And this is what happened. While Persephone lives in the underworld, the days are short and cold. But with her return to Earth in the Spring, the flowers start to bloom, leaves to bud, and the birds sing in the sky.

And then, in a similar way, the archetype of comedy is provided by myths to do with summer, with marriage or triumph; the archetype of tragedy is set by autumn myths, to do with sunset and dying; the archetype of satire comes from winter myths, from darkness and dissolution. In this scheme you can place stories like the fall of Adam and Eve in the autumn phase, the archetype of tragedy.

The point of this is not to initiate a debate over literary criticism but to suggest that there are interesting ideas to explore in relation to corporate identity. Identity can be – often is – misused as a covering over of cracks with a glossy surface texture. But a genuine approach to identity reaches deeper into a company and this is where the idea of story can be revealing.

In the same way that in our collective and individual unconscious we carry an idea of stories – as explained by Jung – I believe that there are also narrative wells from which companies can draw. The stories in these wells form the corporate unconscious, in effect the springs of the company's identity.

This gives depth and breadth to a company's idea of itself. Behind a slogan like **Just do it** there seems to me a wealth of real and potential stories – parent and child, athlete and coach, triumph out of disaster, the sheer joy of achieving a desperately desired goal, the compulsion of commitment. Nike have now started to draw on that well, as in their series of adverts in football programmes based on real stories by real people. This is a well we don't really acknowledge let alone tap. But perhaps companies with strong identities have always done so intuitively.

The most explicit use of the word 'story' in discussing matters of branding and identity has been in Mark Leonard's Demos paper on *Britain*™. In that he suggests six stories which are, in effect, the fundamentals of a new brand for Britain. He describes the stories as *Hub UK, United Colours of Britain, Creative Island, Silent Revolutionary, Nation of Fair Play, Open for Business.*

With the booksellers Waterstone's we have something more than a limited number of stories. Because all of literature and all of storytelling is available in the products sold in Waterstone's, the company's identity emerges through the words, stories and inspiration of books – books classic and modern, famous and unknown, fiction and non-fiction.

Through the use of quotations taken from these books we have been able to demonstrate the central idea of the Waterstone's identity – the celebration of books. We have quotations as a core element of the identity, and then we use an infinitely flexible copy line – whose only fixed words are 'at Waterstone's' – to make clear the link between books and the limitless possibilities that they open up. As I also wrote about Waterstone's:

'A shop with ideas on every subject under the sun'

"Only connect"
E.M.Forster Howards End

Books to make connections
at Waterstone's

" To see a World in a grain of sand "
William Blake
Auguries of Innocence

Books to enrich your life
at Waterstone's

"A snapper up of unconsidered trifles"
William Shakespeare
The Winter's Tale

Books to snap up
at Waterstone's

"Reader I married him"
Charlotte Brontë
Jane Eyre

Books to spend your life with
at Waterstone's

"A circle
is the longest
distance to
the same
point"

Tom Stoppard
Every Good Boy Deserves
Favour

Books that make a point
at Waterstone's

"A green
thought
in a green
shade"

Andrew Marvell The Garden

Books to colour your thoughts
at Waterstone's

"We keep
passing unseen
through little
moments of
other people's
lives"

Robert M Pirsig
Zen and the Art of
Motorcycle Maintenance

Books to catch the moment
at Waterstone's

"The
nowness
of everything
is absolutely
wondrous"

Dennis Potter Interview with Melvyn Bragg

Books for now
at Waterstone's

Waterstone's are at ease with the association with fine writing. Other companies are more ambivalent. In the mid 1980s the industrial finance company 3i had commissioned Christopher Logue to write a poem for them.

Come to the edge.
We might fall.
Come to the edge.
It's too high.
COME TO THE EDGE!
And they came,
And he pushed,
And they flew.

For a company committed to encouraging entrepreneurs it was perfect. But, until we rediscovered it for them more than ten years later and started using it again, it had disappeared from 3i's sight. Why was that? No doubt it was something to do with a gap between aspiration and reality – but also it revealed a fundamental doubt that runs through business life. It raises a question like 'Is it too fanciful?' People equate poetry (and perhaps storytelling too) with qualities that they don't comfortably associate with business fundamentals – imagination, passion, intellect, playfulness.

But is it sane to exclude such qualities from business life? Should we not be nurturing them as ways to show that individual companies have individual differences? After all, some companies succeed by encouraging imagination to develop. More and more, as I work with companies, they are yearning to be more than just an organisation focused on delivering numbers. They want to be seen as risk-taking, creative, entrepreneurial – otherwise they are too grounded in the reality of simply earning a living.

'The new corporate contract is that we'll offer you an opportunity to express yourself and grow, if you promise to leash yourself to our dream, at least for a while.'

John Scully, *Apple*

We express our dreams through images and words. A writer has a special relationship with his words – we feel paternal towards them but we know that they will go out in the world and leave us, most of the time hardly looking back. Through words and through images we are constantly trying to recreate the vividness of a dream, but dreams are never possible to pin down.

John Berger said that 'Visual art is a chase after the invisible'. Equally literary art is a chase after the unsayable. We're always striving to say what cannot actually be expressed in words.

It's there in our heads, often fleetingly, frustratingly, like a dream, but we never achieve an expression of the thought that is perfect. Hemingway made a similar point and we used his words as part of our Waterstone's celebration of literature.

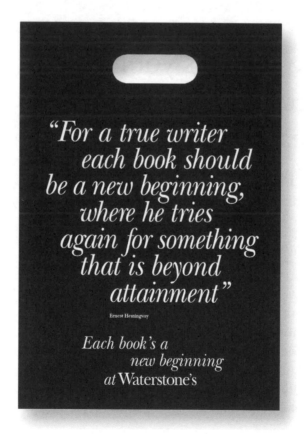

"For a true writer each book should be a new beginning, where he tries again for something that is beyond attainment"

Ernest Hemingway

Each book's a new beginning at Waterstone's

In the end it all comes back to the question of identity.

'I'm a writer. I put words in other people's mouths.'

Dennis Potter, *Cold Lazarus*

Writers put words in other people's mouths, even when they are supposedly our own. It reminds me of the story of a US sitcom where the star of the show played himself. The scriptwriters decided for one episode to introduce his twin brother, still played by the same comedian. The problem was that the star of the show got furious and pulled the plug on the episode. Why? *Because his twin brother got all the laughs.*

When we perform – and here I count writing as an act of performance – we all want to be applauded for what we are. Yet we're all aware that the act of performance transforms us into someone close to but interestingly different from ourselves.

The trick is to learn to enjoy the performance.

Let your twin brother have the laughs.

So, in the end, what does this come down to? Simply that identity is a subject of extraordinary complexity that cannot be reduced only to the simplicity of graphic marks – no matter how important these outward signs are as reflections of inner being. What matters is the totality of the means we use to reflect the personality – corporate or individual – that lies within.

As companies we have our stories. As individuals we have our stories. From a brand's viewpoint, the stories comprise not only the content, the message, the 'it' of my title, but also the style, the way you tell the story, the tone of voice. These help to make the brand what it is. The writer's role is to express these stories in a way that will convey truth, meaning and insight – and in ways that will engage the attention and affection of different audiences. After all, it's better to be known and liked than simply to be known.

5 FINALE

'So much of a novelist's writing, as I have said, takes place in the unconscious: in those depths the last word is written before the first word appears on paper. We remember the details of our story, we do not invent them.'

Graham Greene, *The End of the Affair*

Have I said what I wanted to say?

I try not to kid myself. This book is not, as they say, 'rocket science'. It is dealing with issues that are close to you and me, it is simply about the way that we communicate with each other.

We do that with words.

It's inescapable. Of course, we communicate through each of the senses and there are people who, for example, will make claims for the transforming power of aroma. I have no intention to denigrate the influence of any of these forms of sensual therapy but for most of us, for most of the time, the way we think and the way we communicate is through words.

That has been the thesis of this book. If you haven't spotted that by now you really haven't been paying attention.

Throughout the book I have freely used quotations from other writers. I have called these writers to witness deliberately, not because they directly support any argument I might wish to make, but because they provide interesting insights into the subjects I have wanted to discuss.

Take the Graham Greene quotation, for example, which stands at the gates of this chapter. As I approach the end of the book, a little like a track runner hearing the bell, I feel a sense of exhilaration that I will complete this particular trial. In writing that, I wonder how will you interpret that word 'trial'? Indeed, how did I intend the word? Did I mean it, following the running analogy, simply as an equivalent of 'event'? Or was it meant to be a more laborious effort than that? Does it have to have connotations of 'tries hard, but could do better'?

In short, what do you really mean by the words that you use?

The fact is that we are less in control of our words than we ever like to think. You start out trying to be an anarchist but end up complaining that other people do not follow the rules. It seems to be inevitable in the cycle of life. As I wrote at the beginning of the book, words take on a life of their own – even if we create them, we have no power over them once they are out there in the world. I am reminded of the formula that President Reagan's minders developed to gloss over his gaffes: 'The President mis-spoke'.

The fact is, we all mis-speak. That is the trouble with words, and also their absolute joy. Words, if we are honest, betray not only what we are really thinking but also what we are feeling in the deepest recesses of our being. There is no point in trying to use words as a defensive shield because they will betray you, they will point towards your vulnerable places. They are reflections of you. They will drive you to the grave or, at the very least, you will take them with you. As Tom Waits suggested for his gravestone epitaph: 'I told you I was sick'.

But who are you? That is easier said than defined.

245

You are all different. Glory in the difference. Whether you are an individual or whether you see yourself as a representative of a company or a brand – glory in the difference. Do not retreat into trying to sound like everyone else. You can, through the words that you use, give a distinct sense of difference to yourself and your company.

I have talked about 'we, me, them and it'. This is about understanding that it, your message, is not simply a factual receptacle. It changes as it is seen through a number of different perspectives: the corporate (we), the personal (me), the audience (them). The message is never purely factual. It is tempered by these different viewpoints. Compare it, if you like, to a visit to the opticians: as your eyes are tested, different lenses are slotted in until you arrive at the sharp image that provides the right vision. When you have that vision right – through corporate, personal and audience viewpoints – you have a distinctive, sustainable tone of voice.

I have ended up talking about tone of voice in terms of vision. Most of my career has been based on the fusion of words and imagery and I believe that, in the end, the two are inextricable. Each supports the other and that is why this book, a book about the importance of words, has relied heavily on the visual to make its points. Put together the visual and the verbal and you have a powerful combination that starts to add up to a brand. And a brand is simply about achieving differentiation, so we need to use these two media – visual and verbal – in combination to achieve that objective.

It comes down to emotion and I am happy to make a passionate plea for the value of emotion in achieving commercial objectives. Recently I wrote a review of the London International Festival of Theatre (LIFT) for a creative industries magazine. In that review I wrote of emotions ranging from childlike wonder to absolute exhilaration brought on by seeing outstanding performances. Now these are emotions you don't often get at work. But we would all work better if we were able to bring this greater range of feeling into those places where we are engaged in what we like to call creative work. Clients are certainly looking for that kind of subversion of expectations.

Don't forget to take yourself to work today.

The ability to write well is the most neglected skill in business life. We all intuitively know that we need to use words well to succeed in our work, yet we continue to regard writers as specialists on the fringes of life. My contention is that writers are thinkers. Good writers are good thinkers. What business does not need good thinking at its heart? If you improve the writing ability of your company, or at least its sensitivity to language, you will improve your company's performance.

It's not, then, a 'nice to have'.

I think not, but I am biased. I have always approached the serious business of thinking by writing, and not everyone has the same inclination. I believe more people have that inclination than we generally acknowledge but I concede that a passion for writing is not a business skill that can be easily achieved by signing up to the equivalent of a Dale Carnegie course. I have been fortunate because I have loved words and have been able to use that love to improve not only my own business effectiveness but the commercial performance of many companies and organisations.

Which is nice.

Yes, but it is also something to be grateful for. Let me conclude on this thanksgiving note by recalling two anecdotes. One of my earliest memories of working life is of being blessed by Robert Maxwell. I was working at one of his companies in the early 1970s, just as it was being taken over by an American corporation – much to Captain Maxwell's distress. He called all the staff together into the company's lecture theatre, gave a rousing but tearful speech and ended by saying 'God bless you all!'

But I don't want to end on a tear. I would rather end on a more purely joyful note which is exactly the way the National Theatre ended its performance of *The Mysteries*. I watched the three parts of this trilogy in the spring of the new millennium. *The Mysteries* were medieval tellings of the Bible stories – the Nativity, the Passion and Doomsday. Watching the performances – particularly as a promenader on the floor of the theatre among the actors – you felt a growing sense of kinship with the cast and the audience. I became part of 'we' as well as 'them', and indeed the lines between each became totally and joyously blurred. At the end of the performance, spectators and performers were one, as each mingled with the other on the stage.

I found myself standing next to David Bradley, the actor who had played God in all three parts of *The Mysteries*. We stood facing each other and applauding. I touched him on the shoulder and found myself thanking God (whose name was David Bradley). And David Bradley (whose name was God) simply said, 'No. *Thank you.*'

There is much to be said for gratitude and for politeness. **Thank you for reading.**

DARK ANGELS

A journey of exploration into writing that's more creative and human

Founded in 2004 by writers John Simmons, Jamie Jauncey and Stuart Delves, Dark Angels has grown from a pilot residential course with no name to a three-tier programme. It offers a unique creative journey developing personal and business writing within a supportive community of writers, in congenial and inspiring retreat settings in Scotland, Northumberland, Spain and Oxford.

In 2015 John, Jamie and Stuart invited eight Dark Angels alumni to join them in delivering the courses, with a view to enriching the sources of inspiration and diversity of practice as well as extending in time to other parts of Europe, USA and Australia.

Foundation courses take place at Highgreen Manor on the Northumberland moors and The Scottish Writers' Centre, Moniack Mhor, in the hills above Loch Ness.

You can find out more here *www.dark-angels.org.uk*

'Dark Angels workshops are uplifting and provocative. Expect to be inspired and forever changed as a writer.'

Richard Pelletier, US writer

LEAVES, a novel by John Simmons

'**Years of experience, wisdom and feeling have gone into this unique story .'**

Elise Valmorbida, novelist,

Madonna of the Mountains

'**John Simmons is the best writer you think you haven't read. In fact, he is one of the architects of the language of our daily lives. With his novel Leaves the secret is now out.'**

Caroline McCormick, former Director, PEN International

'**The phrase a writer's writer is overused but in John Simmons case it is spot on: his sentences gleam and compel you to follow them.'**

John Mitchinson, co-founder QI and Unbound

Leaves was John Simmons' first published novel (in 2015). It was then followed into print by two more novels; all three are now published by Bloodhound Books and available in paperback or Kindle. The connection between writing for business and personal/fictional writing was explored in *We, Me, Them & It* – you can find out the results by reading:

Leaves – a powerful drama about the passage of time

Spanish Crossings – a gripping novel about love, loss and hope

The Good Messenger – a compelling drama about love and deception

A collection of poems *Season's Greetings* is also available in a limited edition. More information about all these and John Simmons' other books on writing for business: www.dark-angels.org.uk

Acknowledgements

I would like to thank the following for the use of extracts reproduced in this book. Tom Stoppard *The Real Thing* published by Faber and Faber Ltd. David Ogilvy *The Unpublished David Ogilvy* published by Sidgwick & Jackson. Gabriel Garcia Marquez *Love in the Time of Cholera* published by Alfred A Knopf, a division of Random House Inc. Anthony Burgess *Earthly Powers* © Estate of Anthony Burgess. David Kusnet *Speaking American* published by Thunder's Mouth Press. Keith Waterhouse *On Newspaper Style* published by Viking. Raymond Carver *Poems* and *Where water comes together with other water* from *All of us: the collected poems*, first published in Great Britain in 1996 by Harvill, copyright © Tess Gallagher 1996, reproduced by permission of The Harvill Press. Also reprinted by permission of International Creative Management Inc. Christian Aid poster, thanks to Partners BBDH. Rob Long *Conversations with my Agent* published by Faber and Faber Ltd. Samuel Beckett *What is the word* © Samuel Beckett Estate, published by Calder Publications. WB Yeats *He Wishes for the Cloths of Heaven* by permission of AP Watt Ltd on behalf of Michael B Yeats, published by Scribner. Wendy Cope *An Argument with Wordsworth* from *Serious Concerns* published by Faber and Faber Ltd and reprinted by permission of the Peters Fraser & Dunlop Group Ltd. *The Only Poem* © Leonard Cohen. Used by permission / All rights reserved. Gwendolyn MacEwen *Let me make this perfectly clear* permission for reprint granted by the author's family. Deborah Gildea of Royal Mail, Tim Clarke of Anglia Railways, John

Dodds of Air Products & Chemicals Inc, Alex Butler of
Cable & Wireless for allowing me to reproduce work
carried out for them. Timothy O'Grady and Steve
Pyke *I Could Read the Sky* first published in 1997 by
The Harvill Press. Text copyright © Timothy O'Grady
1997. Reproduced by permission of The Harvill Press.
Dennis Potter *Cold Lazarus* published by Faber and
Faber Ltd. Douglas R Hofstadter *Le Ton beau de Marot*
published by Bloomsbury Publishing. Javier Marias
A Heart So White first published in 1992 by Editorial
Anagrama, Barcelona. First published in Great Britain
in 1995 by The Harvill Press. Copyright © Javier
Marias 1992, copyright © Editorial Anagrama SA 1992.
English translation © The Harvill Press. Reproduced
by permission of The Harvill Press. Tom Peters *The
Tom Peters Seminar* published by Macmillan. Michael
O'Mara for *Diana: Her True Story in her own Words* edited
by Andrew Morton. Steve Bell from *If ...* published
by the *Guardian*. Christopher Logue for his poem for
3i. Graham Greene *The End of the Affair* published
by Heinemann. Strenuous efforts have been made to
contact all copyright holders and we apologise if any
have been inadvertently overlooked.

We, me, them & it

Index